Presented to: My Dearest
Friend & Sister in Christ,
Ella Wright.

I WANT THAT MOUNTAIN!

Let us get that mountain
and Praise the Lord for
our Victory! Amen!
Note: Continued in back fly leaves.
From: Marian Robinson in
Christian love.

Note: Continued in book 29/30

I WANT THAT MOUNTAIN!

by

G. AVERY LEE

THOMAS NELSON INC.
NASHVILLE / NEW YORK

Library of Congress Cataloging in Publication Data

Lee, G. Avery.
  I want that mountain!
  Includes bibliographical references.
  1. Mountains in the Bible. 2. Baptists—Sermons. 3. Sermons,
American. I. Titles.
BX6333.L395I22   248'.48'61   74-13017
ISBN 0-8407-5582-1

To Gladys

CONTENTS

PREFACE

The episodes of Israel's history that took place on some mountain have, I think, something to say to us. Each of the experiences revealed something more of God. In these chapters, I have tried to catch the mood of the immediate scene and then see what eternal truth there might be in that timely situation.

The study has been immensely rewarding and personally enriching, but more difficult than I first thought. In some cases, the material has been overabundant; in others it is very sparse. This has called for selectivity on the one hand and imagination on the other. Chapter one sets the stage and establishes the mood. The "mountains" have not been arranged in chronological sequence.

I have drawn from many sources. Proper credit has been given where possible. Where ideas have been "borrowed," I have stated the source, if not the specific location. A part of what has been read and remembered, without earlier notation, is not easy to document; so apologies are offered for omissions.

My thanks and appreciation go to Mrs. George (Valerie) Pierce, my secretary, for typing the manuscript.

G. Avery Lee
New Orleans, Louisiana

ix

I WANT THAT MOUNTAIN!

CHAPTER ONE

I WANT THAT MOUNTAIN!

JOSHUA 14:6–15

"Now therefore give me this mountain."
(Joshua 14:12)

There is something fascinating and awe-inspiring about the mountains. Those of us who grew up on the Southwestern plains or live in the Southern swamps and bayous find it difficult to understand the strange attachment that the mountains have for those who dwell among them. For us, God's hand rests in other places; were I to retreat for meditation, it would be to the banks of the mighty Mississippi River, there to watch the flow of "The Father of Waters," a flow as eternal as the moon's rising, as timeless as the love of God.

Nevertheless, when we flat-landers see the mountains, we, too, are impressed and inspired. There is the majesty of the rugged mountains of New England. There is the inspiration of the Great Smokies in North Carolina; the Christian assemblies of Ridgecrest, Montreat, Junaluska, or Blue Ridge were not located in those lovely mountains by mere accident. There is the bleak beauty of such individual peaks as El Capitan out near Van Horn, Texas. And Alaska. Ah, the exqui-

site beauty of Mount Juneau by moonlight! Switzerland
has nothing to compare with it.

Surely, God must be in the hills. I am indebted to a
friend, Dr. Charles A. Trentham, for a special insight.
Dr. Trentham once began an opening-of-school sermon
at the First Baptist Church of Knoxville, Tennessee with
these words:

I never like to begin my ministry to the shining company
of young people who gather here from all over the nation
without retreating for a few days into the mountains.

Not many nights ago, after darkness had come down, I
looked out over the plunging valleys—shadowed by mountains that are older by millions of years than the Rockies,
Cascades, or Sierras—and in that moment, the Creator gave
me a parable. A strange and narrow shaft of golden light
emerged from the thick darkness. Slowly the moon was
rising above the black mountain and the orb of wonder and
romance was once more walking in the heavens.

All day long I had been wondering what new thing I might
say to the freshmen who would appear in this house of God
for the first time. The parable was the answer. The moon
has been coming up for millions of years over those same
mountains. Night after night millions of eyes have seen it.
Each new rising was a miracle of wonder as great as though
it had never happened before. That is the way of the truth
of God. It is forever old and forever new.[1]

On High Places

People like to build on high places. In ancient times
it was often for defense, but it was more. To the

devout Jew, Zion was a city set on a hill, much like his beloved Jerusalem, the Holy City, built on hills. The Greeks built on the Acropolis, the high place; that's where the Parthenon is. The Romans established "The Eternal City," Rome, on seven hills. Cities, colleges, churches, and other landmarks are more often found on a hill than in a valley. Of course, the valley is important because it is beautiful, peaceful, and productive. But when one looks to the mountains, there is challenge. Someone has said that, since man found God on a mountain, and now seems to have lost God, he keeps hoping that by returning to the mountains he will find the God he has lost . . . or forsaken.

Mountains Make Men

Much has been written about the bearing of geography on the character of people: the encircling sea on the history of Britain; the great forest on the making of the peasants of Russia; the climate on the character of the Spanish people; the energy of those who live in the colder climates; and the languid quality of the South Pacific islanders. George Adam Smith, in *The Historical Geography of the Holy Land,* developed the subject with special reference to the religion of the Jews. He showed, for example, how, unlike that of Egypt, the climate of Palestine suggests "a personal Providence." He could have written a chapter, perhaps even a volume, on the hills and mountains of the Holy Land.

There is a peculiar affinity between people and hills. As one well-known mountain climber expresses it, there is:

Some quality in a hill which defies analysis. Call it the
spirit of the hill, call it anything you like, but no one has
yet explained why it is hills have a power over men, why
artists and poets find in them fit subjects for their artistry
and poetry.[2]

In the forty-first chapter of Isaiah there is a fascinating story with two sharply contrasting sentences: "You
worm, Jacob . . . I will make you a threshing sledge"
(Isaiah 41:14–15). The supine dejection of the exiles
is contrasted with the triumphant prospect God has
in store for them. "You worm, Jacob!" Devout folk
often seem like crawling, groveling things; their concept of humility is a false one. The church, for example, has too much of a tendency to go underground in
the face of current threats and issues instead of standing
and facing them with courage and daring. God does
offer us help, but He expects and requires an erect
posture on our part.

"I will make you a threshing sledge!" What a trans-
formation! A worm becomes a heavy sledge studded on
its underside with knives or sharp stones. There were
formidable obstacles to be faced, mountains, in fact.
Mountains and hills were often symbols of Israel's foes,
or, more generally, the overwhelming difficulties she
faced. But more often the mountains were symbols of
Israel's strength. A worm is impotent before a mountain,
but a people resolutely committed to God can be em-
powered to cope with anything. Mountains can be
crushed and become gravel; hills can become dust which
the wind blows away.

This odd combination of metaphors—worm and
threshing sledge—describes what God can make out

of his church in a crucial hour. A worm before a mountain; such we often feel in the presence of our problems. But we can become a threshing sledge with sharp teeth when we vigorously exert our God-given powers.

In the scene described in Joshua 14:6–15, Caleb was fully aware of all the difficulties that had not been resolved. Forty years earlier (cf. Numbers 13), Moses had sent him and eleven other men to survey that area. Ten of the men came back with a negative report and a defeatist attitude. They described the land as being occupied by giants, with cities so well fortified that they considered them impregnable.

"We seemed to ourselves like grasshoppers," they said. There was no chance for success in the adventure being planned by Moses.

But Caleb, along with Joshua, presented a minority report. They were as fully aware of the difficulties as the other ten, but they saw possibilities. They believed they could succeed. Said Caleb:

Let us go up at once and occupy it; for we are well able to overcome it (Numbers 13:30).

If the Lord delights in us, he will bring us into this land and give it to us . . . do not fear the people of the land . . . the Lord is with us (Numbers 14:8–9).

He was confident that with God they could prevail, that one day the land would be theirs. But the ten said:

We are not able to go up against the people; for they are stronger than we (Numbers 13:31).

The fearful people sided with the ten; they even asked for someone to lead them back to Egypt. Moses, for once, sided with the majority.

For forty years the children of Israel wandered in the wilderness seeking the Promised Land. Now Moses was gone, and Joshua was in charge. No doubt Joshua remembered that earlier day when he and Caleb were in the minority. The land was still occupied by giants with fortified cities. There were "Golan Heights" everywhere. Caleb was now an old man of eighty-five years. He was aware of the problems. But Caleb was still not afraid to ask for "that mountain" because he believed that, by the grace of God, he would conquer as a threshing sledge.

No one should close his eyes to the inevitable difficulties with which life confronts us at every turn. But however great the difficulty, a stubborn faith in God will one day be vindicated. Notice how the passage ends: "And the land had rest from war" (Joshua 14:15).

Mountains Are a Challenge

Faith in God does not mean an unambitious dead calm of satisfaction with the present. Nor does it mean fear of the future. God is a God of ambition for tomorrow. Faith brings a divine discontent with things as they are and a will to make things what they ought to be. The mountains are a challenge. That mountain that used to throw itself across the path of a people, saying: "Thus far you shall go and no farther," has always been a challenge to men. Men have risen up with a combination of faith and imagination, plus hard work, and said to such a mountain, "We want *you!*"

God made those mountains; and, changeless and waiting, they have been calling endless centuries for men to come and unlock their treasures:

Stored-up fuel.

Pent-up power.

Locked-up treasures.

On their sides are mighty forests and stones to be used for building. On the inside is treasure: gold, silver, iron, copper, precious stones, and uranium with which to finance the building and enrich life.

Caleb-like, some man always steps out and says: "While you are choosing the easy places, wanting the security of Egypt, *give me this mountain*. I want it for God!"

So here we stand, not confronting physical mountains, but facing great heaps of possibilities in human beings that cry out for some attention, respect, acceptance, opportunity, and love. We do face mountainous obstacles of every variety:

War.

Poverty.

Racial tensions.

Environmental pollution.

Population explosion.

Ecological imbalance.

The drug culture.

People searching for some meaning in life, some purpose for life.

On both the domestic side and on the international level, we face giants which are seemingly impregnable. Let us not think of ourselves as worms or grasshoppers; let us have the confidence of Caleb that causes us to become threshing sledges.

We Need No Weak Religion

Weakness is always inclined to worship strength. We humans are much like a vine, wanting something to cling to that is stronger. The world has no use for a weak God. The world can never cling to a weak religion. The God of the mountains is a God of strength. Martin Luther rallied a generation facing obstacles as great, or greater, than ours by singing, "A Mighty Fortress Is Our God." Our generation needs that kind of conviction and assurance.

One of the sad things about much of today's religion is its facile sentimentality about the brotherhood of man that forgets the fatherhood of God. It lacks stability because it lacks strength. Religion is a beautiful ideal: a vision splendid, a peace that passes understanding. But that's not all it is. As someone put it, "Nothing before and nothing behind, the steps of faith fall on the seeming void and reach the rock."

Let us see if we can get an understanding of what is meant in Psalm 121. Perhaps written by one of the Babylonian exiles, looking not actually, but with hope and idealism to those mountains round about Jerusalem, the Psalm says: "I lift my eyes to the hills. From whence does my help come? My help comes from the Lord, who made heaven and earth" (Psalm 121:1-2).

The psalmist could not see the mountains, but they are there—those hills and that God. Maybe he remembered them from childhood, or had been told about those mountains and that God. He knew about Moses, Joshua, and Caleb. His religious faith went back to the God who gave birth to those mountains. Such religious faith, though rock-ribbed and granite-based, is not a religion of austerity but of strength.

Fixed as the Mountains

Our restless, searching generation tells us that there is no certainty in religion; that there is nothing to faith; that there is no assurance of God. Let us not be exasperated with them, nor angry at them. They have listened to some strange voice and responded to some vague promises. We need to show them the validity of our faith and demonstrate to them that some things are as fixed as the mountains. And God is certain.

The hills and mountains were closely associated with the great events in the history of Israel. Nearly all of the outstanding personal and dramatic experiences seem to have been connected with mountains. Among the hills, Israel learned just about everything that made her mighty as a spiritual power.

Mountains

It is enough here to mention that at Mount Sinai the wandering tribes, entering into a covenant with God, became a nation, and received the Ten Commandments.

Moses was called in the high places and at last died on top of Mount Pisgah (Nebo).

Saul and Jonathan were slain on Mount Gilboa after Saul sought vainly for the lost will of God. Elijah in an hour of crisis met and confused the priests of Baal on Mount Carmel.

But not only were the hills connected with individual inspiration and dedication, they were often the scene of idolatrous practices against which the prophets of God protested.

The greatness and grandeur of the hills impresses us

again when we pass on to the New Testament story. The Mount of Transfiguration and the Mount of Olives, for example. How fitting that so much of the training of The Twelve took place in quiet spots away from the city. The Sermon on the Mount, with its Beatitudes showing the characteristics of the citizen of the Kingdom of God, and the loftiest ethical teaching to be found anywhere, was spoken on a hillside. And it was on a green hill outside of Jerusalem's walls that the Saviour gave his life.

I, too, *want some of those same mountains* of historic significance, for I believe that the events which transpired on them can give meaning to our modern lives.

Says Carter Helm Jones:

The mountains! The mountains of the Bible! O quivering Sinai of Law! O wondrous Pisgah, on which Moses stood and viewed a promised land . . . O Carmel, . . . which certified the eternal One! O Mount of Olives, Christ-haunted! The mount of love! The mount of the centuries! O mountains of God, and God of the mountains, speak to us today, for from everlasting thou art God.[3]

Wanting any mountain involves some risk. Life itself is a risk. Where there is no risk, where is the thrill in climbing the mountain?

NOTES

1. An unpublished sermon.
2. Smythe, *The Spirit of the Hills,* p. 297.
3. Carter Helm Jones, *Prophetic Patriotism,* Broadman Press, Nashville, Tenn., p. 21.

CHAPTER TWO

MOUNT SINAI—THE LAW OF GOD

EXODUS 20:1–17

"And God spoke all of these words."
(Exodus 20:1)

Among the legends of ancient Israel there is a charming one concerning the Ten Commandments. When it became known that God was about to make the revelation of His law to the people of Israel from a mountain top, all of the mountains appeared before God to plead, each one, that it might be chosen for this great honor.

"Great God of all, choose me," said Mount Hermon, "I am the highest of the mountains. It was my summit which, alone of all, towered above the waters of the flood, even as Thy Torah stands above all the sins of the world."

"Choose me," said Mount Carmel, "for I am lovely as a garden. Plant upon me the truth of Thy Torah, as Thou didst plant the tree of life in the Garden of Eden."

"Choose me," said Mount Lebanon, "for the voice of my cedars sings of Thy greatness, as Thy Torah turns all the storms of the world into music, hymning Thy praise."

But God said to Mount Sinai:

"From thy summit shall my Torah go forth to my

people, for thou art set alone in the desert, even as
Israel is alone among the peoples, even as I, Yahweh,
am alone in the desert of the universe."

Another legend says that at this time God spoke
his law simultaneously in all the languages of the world.

The Sinai Peninsula is a 200-mile-long triangle at
whose Southern apex the Gulf of Acqaba joins the Gulf
of Suez at the head of the Red Sea. Its inverted base ex-
tends 150 miles along the Mediterranean Sea, forming
the border between Palestine and Egypt. El-Arish, the
capital of Sinai (now known as Gaza), is a small town
on one of the world's oldest highways, "The way of the
land of the Philistines," used by the Pharaohs and modern conquerors, including today's Israel.

A Sacred Mountain

Mount Sinai is the name used for a sacred mountain in the region. It is also known as Mount Horeb.
Mount Sinai is repeatedly referred to in the Old
Testament as the awesome elevation where Moses received the Ten Commandments. Several locations have
been suggested for Mount Sinai:

1. Jebel Hellal, which is about 30 miles South of
El-Arish (cf. Exodus 19:16).

2. Jewish scholars incline to identify with the vol-
canic Mount Seir, south of Palestine, not far from
Kadesh (cf. Deuteronomy 33:2).

3. But predominate tradition points to Jebel Musa—
"The Mount of Moses." This tradition dates at least
from the time of the Emperor Justinian (A.D. 527-564),
and fits the scriptural description found in Exodus 19:2
and Numbers 33:16 about "the wilderness that is before Sinai."

Overlooking a valley in the East side of the range, at the foot of Jebel Musa, is the Wadi ed-Deir, 5,000 feet above sea level. There is located the famous Monastery of Saint Catherine, portions of which date as far back as A.D. 330.

Priceless Manuscripts

In 1844 on a visit to the Monastery of Saint Catherine, the German scholar, Konstantin von Tischendorf, in search of old manuscripts, saw a number of vellum leaves in a basket to be used for lighting convent lamps. He was permitted to take 43 of the 129 leaves, all portions of the Old Testament. His enthusiasm caused the suspicious monks to refuse him anything else. Count Tischendorf returned in 1853, but found nothing of value. On a third visit in 1859, as he was about to leave, a steward told him that he had a manuscript of the Septuagint, the Greek translation of the Old Testament. When Tischendor opened the package, to his great joy he found a manuscript of the Greek New Testament. This has become known as the Codex Sinaiticus. It is as near as we can come to the original. The manuscript was sold to the Emperor of Russia. After the Russian Revolution of 1917, the manuscript was purchased by the British Government by public subscription for about $500,000. It is now in the British Museum in London. Mount Sinai is, therefore, forever associated not only with the Old Testament, the Law of God, but with the New Testament, the new Covenant of God.

The Ten Commandments were given to Moses on Mount Sinai. Thirty centuries later the new covenant was found on Sinai. How appropriate—that where the old covenant was given to Moses, there on that

same mountain was found the oldest copy of the new
covenant—a manuscript dating from the fourth or fifth
century, written in Greek, in brown ink, on 326½ leaves
of papyrus.

As already stated, the exact location of Mount Sinai
is disputed. We must admit that we do not know
for certain just where the sacred mountain stood. But
the exact location of Mount Sinai matters little. What
is important is the *event*. Somehow the Hebrews made
their escape from Egypt in a fashion that proved
to them that God was working with them, and *somewhere* they met God. It was then that the real work of
Moses was accomplished. What was done on Mount
Sinai was the establishing of a covenant between God
and Israel. Or, we might better say, between God and
man. Somewhere, sometime, each person must meet God
and establish a covenant. We Christians believe that
this meeting and this covenant is through faith in Jesus
Christ.

The "Covenant Code" (The Ten Commandments) as
a separable unit in the book of Exodus is said to have
been first isolated by Goethe. Of all the codes of the early
Near East it is the only one that has played a continuous
role in the cultural process. Without it, Western Civilization as we know it would not exist. Less than a century ago it was the only code known to exist. Then
others were discovered: The Code of Hammurabi, the
Assyrian Code, the Hittite Code, and the Hurrian Laws.

The relation between the Decalogue and these other
ancient codes is indirect. To be sure, there are some
similarities. Maybe Moses did know something of the
Hammurabi Code. After all, he was educated at the top
level of Pharaoh's court. There are no verbally parallel

laws. Not a single law in the Covenant Code is an exact duplication of the law in the older Code of Hammurabi, for example, although that one may have been written a thousand years earlier.

In telling of the journey from the sea to Sinai, the Old Testament writers show little concern with the empirical facts of geography or history. The harshness and risk of life in the barren desert were pointed up, but there are few details. They were not interested in current history. The purpose is to show that Israel, despite the miraculous character of her deliverance, was still subject to the moral and physical conditions of struggle that all men meet in history. The difference is that the revelation of God gave meaning and direction to the struggle. The desert pilgrimage with its fears and crises is related to convey the teaching that Israel's fulfilment of life in the Exodus is a fulfilment of faith.

For Israel the core of God's revelation was the Exodus, an objective, historical fact. The climax of God's disclosure is the crossing of the sea. This historical occurrence is the cornerstone of Israel's existence as the people of God. The revelation of God has taken place in the Exodus—the deliverance, and joyful and spontaneous testimony is borne to the God who has made himself known. (cf. Miriam's song in Exodus 15:21) Sinai stands for the systematic interpretation of the faith which is the gift of God's revelation. Sinai stresses the organic and living relationship that exists between the social and religious institutions of Israel and the revelation of God.

The Law is recognized as the revealed will of God for his chosen people. The Law provides for almost every situation that could arise between man and God, man and man, man and the animals, even man and the earth, the environment.

But the Hebrew Law has a spirit which makes it uniquely superior to the codes of its neighbor nations. It is more than a document to be obeyed; it is a power which lifts the quality of the life of those who obey it. It is unflinching monotheism, but it has a kindly consideration of all living creatures. Then, and this is important, there was an optimistic realism which enabled the Jews *to reinterpret* their ancient laws in terms of the needs of successive ages. This is something we Christians need to learn: to interpret our faith in each age and never let it become rigidly fixed to the past. To know and to do the will of God was Israel's primary consideration. This should be our concern, too.

Law and Order

In the past few years, we have heard a lot about "Law and Order." The campus disturbances, the ghetto uprisings, racial disturbances, and rising crime statistics have been largely responsible. The 1968 Presidential campaign saw this idea come into some prominence. But it became a major political theme in the 1970 national elections. In fact, some political orators made "Law and Order" the dominant issue.

It is not our purpose here to defend or attack the use or misuse of "law and order" as a political device. I will say, however, if any society is to exist it must have both law and order. To allow every man to be his own "Law West of the Pecos" would lead to chaos, and we would soon have anarchy, which would produce a dictatorship. Some strong group would come into power, and severe restrictions would be placed on everyone. Some laws may be abusive and punitive. Some may show preferential bias. There may be some harassment under the law. And "equal justice under the law" has become a kind of fantasy. But there is such a thing as "due process," and there are legitimate ways of changing laws that are wrong.

Society has to impose certain civil restrictions. That's why all those ancient codes came into being. Of course, law is externally imposed. The internal "law of love" is very difficult to mature into, if anyone ever does. The talk about "the law of love" is too often "love on *my* terms." And it is difficult to see much love in all the "love talk" these days. Too much of it is very self-centered.

Are law and liberty then at odds? Many assume them to be. Law restricts and restrains; liberty sets free. To be able to do exactly as one pleases, that is to be free, or so some seem to think. But, as Thomas Huxley once pointed out, "Man's worst difficulties begin when he is able to do as he pleases," for then he must decide what he pleases to do. Freedom is simply an opportunity for choice; it gives no guidance as to what the choice should be. Saint Augustine put it: "Love God and do as you please." That sounds good, but too many of us put the emphasis on "do as you please" instead of on *love God*.

The Law of God is not the negation of freedom. It is not a limitation on vital living. Rather, it points the direction in which life must flow if we are to fulfill our potential. Restlessness, dissatisfaction, and despair are not the lot of one who lives within God's law; they are the marks of the rebel against God.

Remember, those were primitive times when Moses

was on the scene. He was dealing with people who had
been living in slavery under severe restrictions. Now
they had some freedom. But it could not be "every man
for himself," not if they were going to accomplish anything. If they were to be God's people, some rules had to
be set up, a covenant had to be established. These
were "children," so to speak, who needed some external
guidelines.

Commandments Still Relevant

It would be good to give a full treatment of each of
the Ten Commandments. However, that is not our
purpose here. There are many volumes discussing each
commandment in detail. Suffice it to say about the Commandments: *They are not out of date!* Take a look at
our society, and we can see that. There is no Rich Young
Ruler among us today who can say, "I have kept the
commandments since my youth." Our purpose here is to
see that on Mount Sinai the Law of God was established: what Winston Churchill called "The most de-
cisive leap forward ever discernible in the human
story." [1]

The genius of Israel's existence was her commitment to God, and the covenant which sealed that pact
was the cohesive force that held together the disparate
elements of that early confederacy. Central to the Sinai
Covenant were the stipulations known popularly as The
Ten Commandments, the Decalogue, or The Ten
Words. The Decalogue contains those principles which
were to govern the relationship between God and
Israel. The Decalogue was the foundation of the covenant life. It was not the means of achieving the cov-

enant, for the covenant was an expression of God's grace. The Law served as a net cast over Israel, showing that she was within the bounds of the covenant fellowship.

Apart from the covenant, there is no other way to account for the unanimity with which the Jews regard themselves as belonging to God. The fact that this relationship rested on a covenant had a marked effect on the Jews' attitude toward God. The nations about them looked upon themselves as being bound to their gods by a *natural* tie, like that uniting members of a clan or a tribe. But the Jews were conscious that God had taken them to himself by *free choice*. Voluntarily he had set his love upon them and called them. This kept alive a feeling of gratitude and humility. Also, the Jews had chosen to worship *of their own free choice* in accepting the covenant. To keep the relationship between people and God alive, the covenant must be obeyed . . . voluntarily.

There are many Christians who proclaim, "We are not under Law: we are under grace." To an extent this is true. But, remember, the Law, too, was established under God's grace. There was a new law when Christ came. But Jesus said: "I am not come to destroy the law, but to fulfill it" (Matthew 5:17). The new law of Christ was not a requirement of abstinence or negation. It imposed positive obligations of spirit and deed and gave men forgiveness. The old law was inscribed on tablets of stone; the new law was written on the inmost heart of man.

I believe in the Law of God. I believe the moral, ethical, and spiritual laws of God are every whit as binding and effective as the laws of God's physical universe. Break the physical laws—gravity, for example—and we suffer; cooperate with and work with them, and we achieve—walking on the moon, for example. The same is true with the spiritual laws.

Almost daily I counsel with someone who is a breaker of the covenant. For one thing, *I break it,* and I deal with me. Name any one of the Ten Commandments and within a month I've dealt with someone who has broken one or more of them. I deal with those who do not believe in God,

who take God's name in vain—even cursing God,
who break the sabbath,
dishonor parents,
kill,
commit adultery,
steal, lie, cheat,
and covet.

I know these Commandments *are not out of date.* I know what breaking them does to people emotionally and spiritually.

The Appeal of Authority

I have often puzzled at the visible success of rigid, authoritarian religious groups with firmly fixed requirements to which they require strict adherence. I have long felt that the reason is that people *want to be told* what to do. It's a lot easier that way . . . to let someone else do your thinking and tell you what to do. Children get along better in families where certain regulations are established, where both parents and children know what the rules are. It's hard to be free, to make your own choice, to live under the simplistic law of love. I think it's better, but it is harder.

This was brought home to me in a striking way a few years ago while watching a TV program dealing with a youth movement called "The Children of God." The group was composed of former drug addicts, sexual freedom advocates, black militants, every kind of the "hippie" culture crowd who said they had "found" Jesus, that they were on a "trip" with Jesus. In Jesus, they said, they had found meaning and purpose for life. *And they had!* Something had happened to them that radically changed their lives and set them on an entirely different course.

The strange thing about this cult of "The Children of God" was the extremely rigid rules and the ultra strict conformity: no drugs, alcohol, sex, tobacco; all the decisions made by the "Elders"; the signing away of income; the absolute communal control. These "children" were of the "now generation," rebels against authority and the "establishment," but they had found and responded to a strict authoritarianism. Why? The TV announcer said: "They have found certainty in an uncertain age."

They had changed, no doubt about that, and they seemed sincere. Maybe it wouldn't last. So what? They had found something in the "Law of God." Maybe they would grow and mature in what we would call "The Law of Love."

Some years ago Leslie Weatherhead of London was speaking at the Rayne Memorial Methodist Church in New Orleans. Billy Graham had just concluded his first London Crusade. There was some criticism of Graham, and Weatherhead was asked his reaction. He said something like this: "It is obvious that the churches of England are not reaching the people, not getting them in church. Mr. Graham has reached them and gotten them into church. We will take care of their theology later."

I like that!

The churches had not reached these young people. The "Children of God" movement had. The movement had something that got to them. Let's hope we can have a chance at doing something about their theology.

One thinks as he watches America living prosperously, making technological progress, even advancing a little in human relations that perhaps we are on the way. Then we see those inevitable temptations that play on all of us, causing us to stumble and fall. It is becoming increasingly clear that, if we are really to go forward, we must go back to some fine old things that are basic to human behavior. Many today, especially youth, think they have reached the place where all attention can be fixed on Paul's positive ethic, "Love is the fulfilling of the law," and we can eliminate the negative "Thou shalt not." But some are learning better as they become better acquainted with human life. Those Ten Commandments, that covenant, needs to be emblazoned in every marketplace, every school house, every home, every church.

The thing is, there is such a thing as the Law of God, given by the grace of God. Each of us must come to his own Mount Sinai and respond *of his own free will* and enter into covenant with God. As Christians, we believe this is done through repentance of sin and faith that accepts Jesus Christ as Saviour.

So, I want that mountain of a universe ordered by the law of the Creator, and of life governed by the eternal principles of that same God.

NOTES

1. Winston Churchill, *Amid These Storms,* p. 293.

MOUNT NEBO—THE UNFINISHED TASKS OF GOD

Each Generation Has Its Own Task

*"Look at it with your eyes; for you shall
not go over this Jordan."
(Deuteronomy 3:27)*

The one utter heresy of Christianity is to believe that we have reached finality and can settle down with a completed system. That is an essential denial of the living God, who cannot have said his last word on any subject or landed his last hammerblow on any task.

It is strange that in religion we so desperately try to cling to static, settled, authoritative finality as though some "faith once delivered to the saints" were our safety and strength. In no other realm do we even dream of such an attitude: not in medicine, art, science, or education. In all realms, religion included, human life is creative. It spontaneously wells up into new insights and endeavors. Continuity in any realm of human interest is not to be found in its formulations but in its abiding life.

The spiritual life of man in his relationship to God is an inescapable human interest. Religion is indestructible. But it is an adventure of life and thought, with some action thrown in. All its formulas, summarizing experiences up-to-date, are signposts, not boundary lines. When Christianity forgets that, it becomes preservative instead of creative. It rests in assumed finalities instead of daring new sallies of the spirit. It retreats into supposed citadels instead of taking the open road. It is not only false to its historic origins in the Old Testament—and especially in Jesus Christ, who did the very opposite—but, by psychological necessity, it dooms itself to stagnation and decay.

Unfinished Tasks

There is no better example of the unfinished, ongoing tasks of God to be found anywhere than in this episode of Moses on Mount Nebo.

Sometimes called Pisgah, Mount Nebo is 2,641 feet high. How Moses got to Mount Nebo from the wilderness is a mystery. Today it is approached from the village of Madaba, near the city of Ammon, Jordan. From the top of Mount Nebo one commands a panoramic view of the whole country in every direction. Moses could see the full encampment of Israel. Looking westward, he could see over to what we call the Dead Sea; to Jericho, Bethlehem, and Jerusalem; the Jordan River; and the mountains around Jerusalem. Looking northward, there is the Jordan Valley with the Sea of Galilee and Mount Hermon at the other end.

A church dedicated to Moses, built in the Byzantine era, has recently been excavated on Mount Nebo. It is a thrill for the modern pilgrim to look at the beautiful mosaics that are still visible, the colors only slightly faded.

There was the land of Moses' dreams and aspirations
—*The Promised Land*. He could have sung: "All o'er
those wide, extended plains, I am bound for the promised land." The great panorama was an exhilaration.
And all that water! The most precious of commodities in
that barren wasteland. Once in Israel, looking at the
construction of a huge pipeline, not for oil, but or water,
an Israeli said: "With water we can do anything."
And Israel has made that desert bloom.

So Moses prayed: "I pray thee, let me go over and see
the good land that is beyond the Jordan" (Deuteronomy 3:25).

But God said: "Look at it with your eyes; for you
shall not go over this Jordan" (Deuteronomy 3:27).

Moses could look, but he could not enter. But he was
spared one disappointment: he never knew that the
big sea was salt.

It is pathetic to think of Moses alone on the mountain, viewing the future glory of his people, not allowed
to enter, dying in a strange land, the people mourning
his loss—not even knowing where he was buried so no
shrine could be built. All of this is pathetic, humanly
speaking, and humanly true. But there are implications
in the story that make it distinctive. Moses dies; his
life work is complete; but his hopes, visions, and
expectations for his people are alive.

From the human point of view (which seeks the happy
ending) , we would have preferred the story to end with
Moses triumphantly leading his people over the Jordan
into the Promised Land, a conquering hero.

But there is no need for us to be sad in knowing that
Moses did not get into the Promised Land as such. He at

least saw it. It is quality, not quantity, that makes for
the full life. If God chooses to close a door, no lasting
disappointments can beset a life fully committed to God.
Moses needs no grave or tomb at which the faithful may
gather to preserve his memory.

His work is forever engraved in history, more en-
during than an Egyptian sarcophagus of granite.

Naturally, there was disappointment for Moses. But
no one ever fully completes every task he sets for himself, and surely God has something for someone else
to do. Someone said: "What's the use of starting what
you cannot finish? I hate to start something I cannot
finish." We can understand that, but what about the
one who says: "I do not want to start something I *can*
finish; it would be too small." Can we understand that,
too? The trouble with many of us is that we are too
ready to do the little things we can finish. Some of that
needs to be done, of course. But there is challenge and
adventure in tasks too big for us to finish.

There is always a Joshua who comes after us. Joshua
takes over from Moses and learns that the great body of
water is salt. He learns that each generation faces its
own problems; there are always unfinished tasks of
God.

Nebo is the mountain of vision and disappointment.
It is on Mount Nebo that we hear the last words of
Moses when he pleads with God to let him pass over
Jordan with the people of Israel. We have seen Moses
in some striking and dramatic moments:
When he confronted God in the burning bush,
when he stood courageously before Pharoah,
when he stretched out the rod over the Red Sea,

when he received the Commandments,
when his anger blazed at the Golden Calf and
he smashed those tablets.

But now we see him in one of those tender experiences common to us all: the moment of great personal disappointment. As a Yale professor, Hal Luccock, said shortly before his death: "I don't mind dying; I'd just like to see how it's all coming out." Now at Mount Nebo we see disappointment, but we see more. We see the unfinished tasks of God for some Joshua.

There can be no disappointment where there has been no vision, no aspiration, no desire, no dreams, no effort. Life does have its mountains of success and achievement, but there are also mountains of frustration and disappointment.

Abraham Lincoln was assassinated just when Lee's army laid down its arms, and four years of bloody civil war came to an end. On June 9, 1864, Father Charles P. Chiniquy of Illinois paid his last visit to Lincoln. The President took the Bible from his desk and read those verses in Deuteronomy which tell of the disappointment and death of Moses on Nebo. When he had finished, Mr. Lincoln said:

I have read these strange and beautiful words several times these last five or six weeks. The more I read them, the more it seems it me that God has written them for me as well as for Moses . . . Now I see the end of this terrible conflict with the same joy of Moses, when at the end of his trying forty years in the wilderness; and I pray my God to grant me to see the days of peace and untold prosperity which will follow this cruel war, as Moses asked God to see the other side of Jordan and enter the Promised Land. But do you know that I hear in my soul, as the voice of God, giving me the rebuke which was given to Moses? There is a still, but solemn, voice which tells me that I will see those things only from a long distance, and that I will be among the dead when the nation, which God granted me to lead through these awful trials, will cross the Jordan, and dwell in the Land of Promise . . . It seems to me that the Lord wants today, as He wanted in the days of Moses, another victim—a victim which He has himself chosen, anointed, and prepared for the sacrifice, by raising it above the rest of the people. I cannot conceal from you that my impression is that I am the victim . . . But just as the Lord heard no murmur from the lips of Moses, when He told him that he had to die before crossing the Jordan for the sins of his people, so I hope and pray He will hear no murmur from me when I fall for my nation's sake.[1]

There are many different kinds of disappointment in life. Every life has some disappointment buried within it. The United States Patent Office is full of them. Rejected book manuscripts from would-be authors testify to them. Every family and each individual life has some of them.

What has the Christian faith to say on this very practical subject of life's broken hopes, its frustrated desires, and its disappointments? Two things, at least: First, take them without bitterness; second, disappointments must be considered, not only in the light of the present, but in the light of the future. And this is where "the unfinished tasks of God" come in, where some Joshua appears to lead on.

Religious faith at its source is personal adventure in a way of living. Faith in New Testament days was a matter of personal venturesomeness with Jesus Christ. It was a faith with no formal creeds, for no creeds had yet been written. It was not faith in the New Testament, for the New Testament was not yet in existence. It was not faith in the church, for the church was as yet unorganized. That primary faith which launched the Christian movement antedated creeds, book, and church. It was a personal relationship with Christ and what He stood for. It had not yet been formalized. It was vital and dynamic. It was a continuation of the unfinished task of God. *And it still is!*

What we are saying is that religious faith, Christian faith in particular, is never a finished matter. Why should we ever suppose that it is when the Bible keeps telling us that it is not? As the writer of Hebrews says: "In many and various ways God spoke of old to our fathers; but in these last days he has spoken to us by a Son" (Hebrews 1:1).

The Bible is careful to let us know that at no time has God spoken His last word or called His last person to some final task. To use a phrase again: There is always some new Joshua, because each generation confronts new tasks that are peculiarly its own.

We all know that there is a dangerous alienation of today's younger generation from organized Christianity, that is, the institutional church. There is suspicion that many a young person today who is not a church member, not a Christian, would like to be. Often the churches do not help. Perhaps more often preachers have a way of presenting Christianity as a carefully articulated system of beliefs stiffened into settled finalities. Some even say that the whole complex system of Christian faith stands or falls together, and that one must take it all or have nothing.

Many a youth (and many an adult) who may wistfully desire to be a Christian finds such an approach impossible. He just cannot start with a wholesale acceptance of a finished system. Why should we ask him to when it has taken us, and others, all this time to get where we are? It is as psychologically absurd to expect a youth, as precedent to becoming a Christian, to accept this institutionalized and creedalized bloc called Christianity as it would be to demand creedance of the total college curriculum before allowing a lad to become a freshman.

Jesus' first followers were called disciples—learners, and a learner begins where he is. When Jesus met a man like Zacchaeus, he did not place on him a system of theology and institutionalism. He did not have one. And if he had, Zacchaeus would not have understood it.

Jesus dealt with people one at a time. To no two people did he give the same prescription or formula. He had no predetermined mold into which he tried to pour them all. He had no propositions to which all had to subscribe before they could follow him. He invited each, starting where each was, to begin a spiritual adventure in the unfinished tasks of God.

In the past decade we have been badgered on all sides about "Church Renewal." Even the Roman Catholics got in on the act with Vatican II. After saying the emphasis is needed, the most appropriate remark is that there is very little new about it. The church always needs renewing.

In 1926, Harry Emerson Fosdick was shaking things

up by writing in national magazines about "The New Religious Reformation." In the late 1940's, Clayton Morrison, founder of *The Christian Century,* jarred the ecclesiastical world with a book entitled *The Unfinished Reformation.* Prior to that were men such as Savonarola, John Huss, Martin Luther, John Knox, John Calvin, John Wesley, and William Booth who felt that the church of their day needed to be renewed. As Fosdick put it back in 1926:

Religion, which in its vital origins is like a spring, is continually being cluttered with debris, stopped by its own sediment, impeded by accumulations from without, and the history of religion reveals the necessity of clearing out the spring again and letting its waters flow freely.[2]

The unfinished tasks of God!

The present thrust of "church renewal" seems to be an effort to distinguish the religion *of* Jesus from the religion *about* Jesus. Even this is the exact phrase Fosdick used in 1926.[3]

The contrast between these two types of faith—*of* Jesus and *about* Jesus—throws light on the restless spirit that is now abroad in the churches. The present disturbed condition of America's religious life presents a serious problem.

The failures of old restraints,
   the impotence of old dogmatisms,
      the aggressiveness of impatient radicals,
         the defensive militancy of reactionaries,
            the general confusion and bewilderment
are symptoms of inevitable change.

There is no neat formula that will explain it all and no facile solution that will resolve its difficulties. There is one element in it, however, that is full of promise. There is a widespread, deep-seated, positive desire on the part of many Christians in all our churches to recover for our modern life, for its personal character and its social relationships, the religion of Jesus as distinguished from the accumulated, conventionalized, largely inadequate, and sometimes grossly false religion about Jesus.

Too much so-called conservatism is a negative desire to keep things as they are. Too much so-called liberalism has been conceived in the spirit of protest and expressed itself in denials and attacks. Maybe we could illustrate it by looking at one of the stately old houses on Saint Charles Avenue in New Orleans. The obscurantist wants to keep it exactly as it is; the radical wants to tear it down and erect a modern highrise apartment building. Why not keep its old beauty and functional qualities with a *remodeling* that is *restoration?* Restoration of its original beauty and function, but with central temperature control, a modern kitchen and bath?

This emphasis upon restoring the centrality of the spirit of Jesus in today's Christianity is crucially important if our modern problems are to be successfully met. Here is a new generation needing a vital and dynamic faith as much as any previous generation in human history. There are some unfinished tasks of God, waiting for some Joshua.

Luke begins his second letter to Theophilus by saying: "In the first book, O Theophilus, I have dealt with all that Jesus began to do and teach" (Acts 1:1). Then, in the Acts of the Apostles, he tells of the development of the young church. Jesus had gone, but "new Joshuas" came on the scene, and the adventurous life Jesus began continued.

When magazines used to carry serial stories, each new issue began with a synopsis of what had gone on before—just as TV stories do today. Then there would be this sentence: "Now go on with the story."

The first three books of the New Testament are called "The Synoptic Gospels," summarizing what happened in the life of Jesus of Nazareth. Luke then told us what took place among the early Christians. History brings us up-to-date, then says to us: "Now you go on with the story."

I want that mountain which says, from whatever Mount Nebo we may be on, there is a Promised Land of God out there—an unfinished task of God, waiting for Joshua.

John says to us: "Beloved, now we are God's children; it does not yet appear what we shall be, but we know that when he appears we shall be like him, for we shall see him as he is" (John 3:2).

Fear it, this new unfinished task of God, all those who do not want Jesus Christ to be taken seriously. But no one else need fear it. One of the greatest hours of history will have struck when once more faith in God and Jesus Christ takes the center of the scene.

Notes

1. Quoted by Clarence McCartney, *Mountains and Mountain Men of the Bible,* Abingdon Press, pp. 74–75.
2. Harry Emerson Fosdick, *Adventurous Religion,* Grosset and Dunlap, p. 301.

CHAPTER FOUR

MOUNT GILBOA—MAKING
EXCEPTIONS OF OURSELVES

1 SAMUEL 28:3–6; 31:8; 2 SAMUEL 1:21–27; 21:12–14

"And Saul had put mediums and wizards
out of the land . . . Find me a witch that I
may go and consult her"   (1 Samuel 28:7)

There are two episodes of significance that occurred on Mount Gilboa, that mountain that guards a key pass from the Plains of Esdraelon to the Jordan River, at an elevation of 1,698 feet. Although its western slopes are gentle enough for pasture and safe grazing, its eight miles of rugged terrain make for rough fighting—then and now. The second event, and the one that gets the most attention, is recorded in 1 Samuel 31:8–9: "On the morrow, when the Philistines came to strip the slain, they found Saul and his three sons fallen on Mount Gilboa. And they cut off his head, and stripped him of his armor."

Saul, chosen of God to be the first king of Israel; Saul, with everything in his favor at the beginning, went away from God and lost it all.

To David, although Saul had often sought to kill him, that seemed so terrible a thing that in his magnificent ode lamenting the death of Saul and his beloved friend, Jonathan, he called upon the mountain to mourn:

Thy glory, O Israel, is slain upon thy high places! How are the mighty fallen . . . Ye mountains of Gilboa, let there be no dew or rain upon you, nor upsurging of the deep! For there the shield of the mighty was defiled, the shield of Saul, not anointed with oil (2 Samuel 1:19, 21).

Then, after David became king, troubles arose in Israel, and David began to make amends for the sins of Saul. Finally, David went after the bones of Saul and Jonathan and gave them proper burial. "And after that God heeded supplications for the land" (Samuel 21:14).

The Gilboa episode I want us to consider also has Saul as the central character. It occurred on the eve of the battle with the Philistines in which he was slain.

Saul was having his problems. He had quarreled with the prophet Samuel, who had anointed him king. Now Samuel was dead. Saul had drifted away from God, had lost favor with God, and the problems of the young kingdom multiplied. Earlier Saul had been a zealous reformer who tried to root out from Israel everything that was incompatible with the true religion of God. What we now give the respectable name of "spiritualism"—some contact with the dead—was seen by Saul in the true light of irreligious superstition; so he had outlawed all witches. "And Saul had put the mediums and wizards out of the land" (1 Samuel 28:3). He recognized witchcraft as a public evil and issued an edict against it.

The Philistines were gathered in great numbers to battle Israel, and Saul was afraid. He tried to inquire of the Lord, but there was no answer. So Saul said to his servants: "Find me a witch, that I may go and consult her" (1 Samuel 28:7).

That is one of the most human passages in the Bible—
a man recognizing a public evil as evil, but when the
pinch came, he himself turned that way.

The point of this pathetic story is that Saul had so
lost touch with God and had come to such a pitch of
panic that he was willing to resort to a practice which in
his better days he had condemned. Saul had tried the
permitted orthodox ways of learning God's will and had
failed. The ancient historian is trying to tell us that
Saul did not *refuse* to consult God, but that Saul already
knew himself to be God-forsaken, and in his desperation,
he was willing to try anything to keep his position.

And let us not think Saul too primitive in calling for
the Witch of Endor. Just one of our modern counter-
parts, astrology, should remove the idea of primitivism.
Then, take a look at the revival of witchcraft in England
and in our own nation. Several magazine articles in the
past year and a half have dealt with the subject. Our
enlightened, scientific age is still quite superstitious, it
seems.[1]

Saul made his own rule that all witches and mediums
were to be outlawed. Rightly so. But in his desperation,
he breaks his own rule. How human! Most of us are able
to see the truth and necessity of moral rules. But too
often we apply them to others. We can't understand why
we can't break the rules and not be hurt. We do things
that we know are wrong, and we are unable, or unwilling, to see that our actions harm us. Almost everyone
imagines that he is capable of breaking rules without
being hurt. It is easy for us to see how someone else
needs disciplining, but it is difficult to accept self-dis-
cipline. It's alright for me to fudge on the yellow caution
light at a traffic signal, but it irritates me for the other

fellow to be so careless with my life and car. This attitude, "If you don't like the law, break it," is presently causing us a lot of problems.

Everyone today the word "problem" confronts us. Watching television or reading the newspaper we face such a complicated maze of difficulties that our individual lives seem small, and we feel unimportant in the face of it all.

Suppose there were no problems in the world. What if God had created the universe fully complete and ready for our occupancy, no difficulties to face, nothing new to discover, nothing puzzling to solve, nothing required of us but to settle down and take it easy? Much as we may feel that would be ideal, after a little while of that, can you imagine anything more boring? Instead, God has set us in the wild world of raw materials, given us some guidelines, and let us have a hand in making something out of it. That means that the very essence of life is confronting problems, being waked up by their demands, and doing something about them.

To be sure, there are times when we want to say: "Look, Lord, don't You think You've overdone it with problems so complex that they frighten rather than stimulate?" But in wiser hours, even in a generation such as this one, one can feel the challenge and be stirred. So, as we get a bit older, we can understand what that man about to be beheaded in the French Revolution meant when he said, "It is too bad to take my head off. I wanted to see how all this is coming out." That, at least, is the starting point of a healthy attitude.

We cannot stop there, however. As individuals, small as we are, we are not outside the world like spectators sitting in the stadium watching the action. We are in

the world's game, participants in its winning or its los-
ing, with this question rising for each of us: what is
my place in all this? Or, in a more vital sense, is there
any will of God in it all?

In a deep sense, no one of us can avoid being a part
of the world's problem. "All we like sheep have gone
astray." (Isaiah 53:6). "All have sinned and come short
of the glory of God" (Romans 3:23). There is no avoid-
ing that. Try as we may to do our best, we are sinners,
contributors to and participants in the world's evil.
We moderns have belittled sin and called those who
believe in sin old-fashioned and dreadfully puritanical.
There is a tendency to laugh morality off as a part of
the changing fashion. That is unrealistic, shortsighted
thinking. See what sin really is! Here we are in a world
with difficulties, and the future of our children is de-
pendent on their solution. Sin takes us by the hand and
involves us in the problems.

But, you ask, how can we find anything about the
will of God when we're not even sure that there is a
God, or if there is, that he has anything to offer?

Let's go back and face that temptation to make exceptions of ourselves. Saul did that, remember. Witchcraft is a public evil; so he abolished it. But when his
own bad days came upon him and life closed in, the
old superstition surfaced and he tried to make an exception of himself: "Find me a witch!"

Among us that kind of thing is going on. About
the church, for example, how much do we consult God
or seek witches? Would any of us want to rear our
children in a community where there were no churches?
We recognize that the church problem in America is a
matter of public concern, and that to have the right

kind of churches in our communities, to provide inspiration for private character, and incentive for social service is of first-rate importance. Can we also see that the surrender of those churches to irresponsible leadership, have them deserted by those who should be expected to stand by them so that there is a lapse in that faith which produces character and perpetuates our spiritual heritage, is a public peril?

Yet, in New Orleans, for example, there are at least 100,000 Protestants unaffiliated with *any* church, and at least 50% of those who do belong never attend. Let us ask: are you making an exception of yourself? God and the curch are all right for others; find *me* a witch.

Philosopher Immanual Kant gave us what is called *The Categorical Imperative*: "So act that thou canst will the principle of thine act to be law universal." That is, live so that if everyone lived that way it would be good for the world. Seeing objectively those principles that would make the world a better place, look how we subjectively make exceptions of ourselves.

Drunkenness a national disgrace, but we drink too much.

Narcotics a damaging business, but we let it go on.

Crime a public menace, but the Mafia grows stronger.

Planned obsolescence a drain, but we keep it.

Pollution a detriment to public good, but we tolerate it.

Honesty basic to all business, but we try an undercover deal.

The religious education of our children a national need, but we let our children slide.

In one realm after another, all witches be gone! And

in the next breath, find me a witch! Or as modern
psychology puts it, we rationalize, with endless excuses
dispensing ourselves from obligations we want others to
observe.

Personal Responsibility

Perhaps one reason why we try to escape personal
responsibility is because the world's problems are so big
that what we do seems of no consequence. What does
life matter? What can one person do?

When I was ordained to the ministry in 1937, people
were not interested in public problems. It was the Depression, and we were more interested in the next meal
than in the likes of Hitler and Mussolini. During my
seminary days, the world became engulfed in war. I
became acquainted with what was then called "The
Social Gospel." Some of us who believed in that had to
shout to make ourselves heard. The ardent preacher of
social concern would say: "You there! Trying to
save your own souls, come out of your absorption in your
individual faith and salvation and see the application
of Christian principles to the world at large!"
We're still saying that to many Christians.

But, "the times they are a changin'." There is now a
great interest in public affairs. "How can we help?" is the
cry. Our destiny and that of our children depends upon
solution. We live in a mood of anxious concern about
our problems. So today some of us are beginning to
change our tune. That same preacher would say today:
"You there! So concerned about the world situation, it is
downright hypocrisy in one area after the other to cry
aloud that we must cure mankind's evils when our own

lives are part of the evil to be cured." Let me speak for a moment to you young people, growing up in a generation where the idea of moral law as something eternally true—some things everlastingly wrong and some things always right—has so largely broken down, where standards of right and wrong have become relative, depending upon the situation, and where morality is a matter of doing what you like and what you can get away with without getting caught. All right, so we adults have the responsibility for allowing it to become that way. But what about you; will you keep it that way?

It's My Business

"The way I behave is my own business," is too much the attitude of both adults and youth. But I say, the way we behave is most certainly not our private business; it is the business of us all. Drug addiction, for example, affecting hundreds of thousands, is a national menace, not only now, but to a generation yet unborn. Using drugs is not your own business; it is the business of us all. Saul's seeking a witch when witches had been abolished as a public evil was not a private affair.

A young man comes to see me, terribly depressed about the vile and ugly conditions of the world. He has seen the horrors of Viet Nam and what that war has done to thousands of our finest young men. He is black, so he knows something about that, too. What can I say to him?

Well, I can agree that the world is vile and ugly. I can tell him about other ugliness. For example, in India there were at one time ten million people totally blind and another thirty million partially blind. Those people need not be blind; the causes are known—vitamin deficiencies, no medical care, and the like. A Christian missionary physician, Dr. Victor Rambo, felt compelled of God to go to India and tackle that problem. He felt it could be done. So he began. In the long run, with proper backing and others helping, what would you bet on —the evil, or the solution, when the solution is already at work?

I can also tell my young black friend to look back twenty years, or even ten years, and contrast the situation of black people then and now. Four years ago Fortier High School was 100% white. Today the ratio is about 50 to 50. Yes, there are still problems, a lot of problems. I remind my friends in liberal Madison, Wisconsin, about this when they get uptight about having forty or fifty blacks in their elite high school. Again, in the long run, what would you bet on—the evil, or the solution, when the solution is already at work?

Similar examples can be cited for other problems of the world and our home situation. Not asking for witches, but seeking God and going to work.

Not for a minute can we say that this is easy. It is not easy. For too long we have been glib in saying, "Just find God's will for your life." That is easy to say, but hard to do. Even Jesus struggled to find the will of God for his own life. The most intense scene of personal anguish ever recorded is that description of Gethsemane where Jesus cried: "If it be possible, let this cup pass from me: nevertheless, not as I will, but as you will" (Matthew 26:39). A few hours later on the cross, feeling himself forsaken by God, Jesus did not say, "Find me a witch!" He said: "Father, into Your hands I commend my spirit. It is finished!" (John 19:30) Some twenty years or so ago I came across a little book that has been as meaningful to me as anything I've ever read. Leslie Weatherhead's, *The Will of God,* was written in London against the awful situation of the Nazi bombings. (Published in 1944, I was a bit late in reading it.) Weatherhead divided the will of God into three ideas:

1. The Intentional
2. The Circumstantial
3. The Ultimate

He uses the cross, the crucifixion to show the differences. Was it God's intention, from the beginning, that Jesus should be crucified? At the beginning of his ministry, Jesus does not seem to think so. He came with the *intention* that men should follow him, not kill him. The discipleship of men, not the death of Jesus, was the intentional will of God.

But when *circumstances,* brought on by man's evil, set up such a dilemma that Jesus was either compelled to die or run away, *in those circumstances,* the cross was the will of God. But, remember, those circumstances were the result of man's sin.

When we mean God's *ultimate goal,* the salvation of man, the purpose of God comes to pass in spite of evil. The ultimate goal, our salvation, may be reached by going through evil. In other words, God cannot be defeated! Not everything that happens is God's will, but nothing can happen which defeats his will.

In regard to the cross, God achieved his final goal not simply in spite of the cross, but through it. He achieved man's redemption and thus realized his ultimate will in as full a sense as he would have done had his intentional will not have been put temporarily aside.

What we are talking about is personal conversion—by God's grace to be so inwardly changed that we pass over from seeking the witches of public evil to seeking God.

I want Mount Gilboa to remind me not to go away from God, but to try and keep in his will. I want it to remind me not to try and make an exception of myself, but to recognize that not only am I a part of the problem, but I can also be a part of the answer.[2]

NOTES

1. Read *The Exorcist,* or see the movie.
2. I have drawn from Harry Emerson Fosdick's sermon, "Are You Part of the Problem Or Part of the Answer" for some of the ideas here.

CHAPTER FIVE

MOUNT CARMEL—WHO IS TO BE GOD?

1 KINGS 18

"How long will you go limping with two different opinions? If the Lord is God, follow him; but if Baal, then follow him .... The Lord, he is God" (I Kings 18:21)

One of the most dramatic and exciting scenes in the Bible is Elijah's confrontation with the priests of Baal on Mount Carmel. The sheer, raw courage of one lone prophet of God pitting himself against 450 priests of Baal, backed up by King Ahab and Queen Jezebel, makes for all the intensity of a shootout at No Name City. And our sympathy is with the underdog.

Mount Carmel is a ridge which confronts the Mediterranean Sea on the northwest and the Plains of Esdraelon on the southwest. On its southern side it was (and is) the most fertile strip of land in the entire country. One can drive through that area today from Haifa to Galilee and see its luxuriant fertility and growth.

Because it is visible in all that section of the Holy Land, there is frequent mention of Carmel in the Bible. Even in the Song of Solomon the Shulamite maid is likened by her lover to Mount Carmel:

"Thine head upon thee is like Carmel" (7:5).

In some respects more like a promontory than a mountain, Carmel rises out of the sea at the western end of the Valley of Esdraelon. Although it is not high as mountains go, only 1,810 feet, rising as it does from the plains, it is awesome. The view is extensive and exquisite. At the foot of Carmel lies the chief port of modern Israel, the city of Haifa, a beautiful city which the Israelis call "the city of tomorrow." The sides, all the way to the top, are marked with beautiful modern homes and apartments, with a lovely hotel about half way up. Also about half way up is the golden domed temple of the B'hai faith, which is their international headquarters. From Haifa to Acre stretches the beautiful crescent of the Bay of Acre. The gorgeous azure sea is spectacular, but somewhat marred with modern oil refineries and ships of the world.

But, let's go back to the Mount Carmel of some twenty-eight centuries ago. Here's the situation.

Ahab was the King of Israel. His wife was named Jezebel. To understate the case, neither of them is greatly admired by the biblical writers. Between the two of them they had led Israel into the worship of Baal. The prophets of God were hunted like animals. In the whole nation there were only 7,000 who had not bowed their knees to Baal. Suddenly, the prophet Elijah stands before King Ahab, thundering: "As the Lord God of Israel lives, before whom I stand, there shall be neither dew nor rain these years, except by my word" (I Kings 17:1).

Can you imagine a man praying for it *not* to rain in a land where water was a precious commodity? And it did not rain for three-and-one-half years! Jesus referred to this episode, as did the writer of James. The story was ingrained in Israel's heritage.

The Choice at Mount Carmel

As the Carmel episode begins, the drought is about to end. Ahab had been hunting Elijah all over the kingdom. Now Elijah appears on his own and tells Ahab to gather the people on the slopes of Mount Carmel. Ahab brought 450 priests of Baal. When everyone was assembled, Elijah made his memorable demand for the people to choose between the worship of God and the worship of Baal: "How long will you go limping with two different opinions? If the Lord is God, follow him; but if Baal, then follow him. And the people did not answer him a word" (I Kings 18:21).

Their silence was partly shame and partly indecision. A mind may entertain a host of different intellectual opinions and scientific theories, but religion involves personal commitment. The word "halt" is used in the King James Version, which indicates indecision. The Revised Standard Version uses the word "limping," which is a kind of playing both sides so as not to antagonize anyone—least of all Ahab and Jezebel.

Elijah then challenged the priests of Baal to a trial by fire. Two altars were to be built and two offerings laid upon them. The priests were to pray to Baal and Elijah to God. If the prayers of the 450 were answered by the coming down of fire to consume the offering and the altar, that would show that Baal was God. But if Elijah's prayer brought the fire, that would show that Jehovah was God.

From sunrise till noon Mount Carmel echoed with their cries, "O Baal, hear us!"

But there was no answer, no fire. When they were exhausted and there was a moment of quiet, Elijah, standing on the other side, mocked them. In one of the most exquisite bits of satire and irony to be found in all literature, Elijah mocked them:

Cry aloud, for he is a god; either he is musing, or he has gone aside, or he is on a journey, or perhaps he is asleep and must be awakened   (I Kings 18:27).

The Baalites were stirred to renewed efforts and fervor, and once again Carmel rang with their frenzied shouts. And the gutteral sounds of the Middle East languages make for quite a high decibel rating. Late in the afternoon, they gave up.

Now it was Elijah's turn. In quiet contrast— pianissimo vs. fortissimo, soft-sell vs. hard-sell—he repaired the neglected altar of God. Around the altar he dug a trench and drenched the altar with water, four barrels of precious water. Why, the man must be out of his mind! That must have caused anguished wails . . . seeing water wasted. Then, in one of those sudden deep hushes that often descends upon a crowd, Elijah prayed:

O Lord, God of Abraham, Isaac, and Israel, let it be known this day that thou art God in Israel, and that I am thy servant, and that I have done these things at thy word. Answer me, O Lord, answer me that this people may know that thou, O Lord, art God, and that thou hast turned their hearts back   (1 Kings 18:36–37).

The moment Elijah's prayer was finished, fire came from heaven, consumed the sacrifice and the altar, and licked up the water in the trenches.

Physically speaking, it may have been lightning, since

the long, hot drought of a semi-tropical country naturally ends in a thunderstorm. But to give a natural explanation of the phenomenon does not do away with the miraculous element in it. The real point of the incident is that the lightning, if it were lightning, came at that particular time in direct response to Elijah's prayer. Let's not get bogged down about "natural lightning." The significant fact is that *something happened* there on Mount Carmel which convinced the people that God was superior to Baal. Jesus and James remembered it 800 years later, and here we are talking about it today.

When the people saw this, they fell on their knees and cried: "The Lord, he is God; the Lord, he is God" (I Kings 18:39).

How quickly God can turn the tide of events. In the morning, a whole people guilty of a false worship so firmly entrenched in Israel that it seemed invincible; at sunset, the worship of God restored. When any one of us is disturbed and perplexed at the sway of evil, the success of evil systems, and the strutting of evil men in the world, let us not forget that God is still in charge. The last act is always his.

To give them the benefit of the doubt, the people of Israel had not officially decided to worship Baal, although, practically speaking, many of them had. Elijah called upon them to make a formal decision. The people were silent at first. Why? Well, no matter how entangled they were in the worship of Baal, they were not ready or willing to say that he was God. For that matter, *who is?* They just did not want to antagonize anyone, least of all Ahab and Jezebel, especially Jezebel. *Who does?* We know in our inmost being that the Baals we follow are not God, not worthy of our allegiance and commitment. But we follow them. We need grace and courage to choose and follow God.

Elijah's demand for choosing who is to be God is reminiscent of a scene some 500 years earlier when Joshua said: ". . . if you be unwilling to serve the Lord, choose this day whom you will serve . . . as for me and my house, we will serve the Lord" (Joshua 24:15). The matter of choice is a constant, not a settled thing. Every generation is called upon to make its choice. One of my favorite hymns is James Russell Lowell's "Once to Every Man and Nation." Listen to the words.

> Once to every man and nation
> Comes the moment to decide,
> In the strife of truth with falsehood,
> For the good or evil side.
> Some great Cause, God's new Messiah,
> Offering each the bloom or blight
> And the choice goes by forever
> 'Twixt the darkness and that light.
>
> Though the cause of evil prosper,
> Yet 'tis truth alone is strong;
> Though her portion be the scaffold,
> And upon the throne be wrong;
> Yet that scaffold sways the future.
> And, behind the dim unknown,
> Standeth God within the shadow
> Keeping watch above his own: [1]

Today is a time of decision both for men and nations, just as it has always been. Momentous and far-reaching are the choices now being made. It has ever been thus. We must choose for ourselves. The choices made by those before us do not bind us, even if we are having to suffer some consequences and undo some wrong choices. The past has led us to the present. But the future lies in the direction we now choose to go. In spiritual relationships too many of us flirt, but do not marry; pay courteous attention, but do not decide; give a respectful hearing, but take no risk. With too many, nothing is ever concluded; everything is always left open-ended. But this does not go on forever. We must someday choose—*for or against*. And, as one man put it:

"How many choices does a man get?"

That choice is urgent and need not be labored. We all know that something is wrong with our world and the people in it. Most of us do not desire to continue in the direction we are going because we fear the ultimate destination. It has been felt for some time that the church has not been reaching people for God and Christ. It is disturbing to see the rapid rise of militant anti-Christian movements, as well as general apathy, in lands once considered to be Christian. In half a century, see the growth of Communism in what was once called Holy Russia.

After World War I, look at the rise of Nazism in the land of Luther and fascism in Catholic Italy.

After World War II, observe the second largest Communist Party in the world emerging from the land of the Pope.

Even in the United States, "Christian America," who could say that we are *Christan?* A bit more than 50%

of our people are even nominally connected with a church, and half of them never attending. We are faced with much the situation Elijah faced: People not formally denying God, but practically worshipping Baal.

We dare not drift; we must choose. Decision and commitment are the very essence of personality. To make no choice is the worst possible choice. Men do choose, although they may say they do not. It is in our decisions that the direction of our life is determined. History is but the recording of the results of human choices. The past decisions of our fathers—good or bad—have brought us to this hour. Where we go from here depends on us.

Yes, this issue involves the matter of man's free will. Man must choose, but he can choose the best or the worst for himself. This freedom of choice is at once a beautiful and a dangerous thing. It is like putting a sharp knife in the hands of a child. It can injure, if wrongly used. But we are unable to divest ourselves of the responsibilitiy which goes along with this freedom.

The Bible is full of the recognition of the responsibility of each man for his choice. In the beginning, in the Eden story, everything revolves around the ability of Adam to choose for himself and to assume the responsibility. Invitation always implies the possibility of resistance. If an invitation can be accepted, it can also be rejected.

Jesus, in addressing men, always assumed this freedom. Note his use of such phrases as: "Follow me . . . come unto me . . . come after me."

From this idea of freedom of choice, let's pass to the sentiment of Joshua: "If you will not serve God, then choose whom you will serve." And of Elijah: "How long will you go limping with two different opinions? If the Lord is God, follow him; but if Baal, then follow him." And centuries later the same alternative was put by Jesus: "No man can serve two masters."

If it seems not good for you to choose God, to follow Christ, whom, then, will you follow? All that is opposite? Pleasure that fritters away? Money which comes and goes? Power which corrupts? Indulgences which degrade? Self-will which destroys? Who, or what, is to be the source of all you hope for if you do decide against God and Christ?

To meet Jesus Christ is to stand at the forks of a road to desire all that he offers, and be done with all that offends him. The two aspects of the human act of response to Christ are called faith and repentance; repentance is turning from the road that leads away from Christ; faith is the act of commitment to the road which leads to him.

We cannot ignore or escape Christ. We are coming increasingly to realize that we cannot deny him and his ideals of love, humility, brotherhood, commitment to the will of God, and sacrificial service to mankind; that is, unless we are willing to face disaster in the world of our outer social relations and chaos in our inner selves.

When Joshua put the matter up to Israel: "The people answered him and said, God forbid that we forsake the Lord." When Elijah put the choice before Israel: "The people answered him not a word," although a few hours later they said: "The Lord, he is God." Wilberforce, the great English liberator, had as his motto: "Whatsoever others do, as for me, I will serve the Lord." What one of us does not even now get a thrill when we hear Patrick Henry's "I care not what course others may take, but as for me, give me liberty or give me death." What a phrase, that *as for me!*

But the climax to Elijah's conflict is yet to come. Even after the victory on Mount Carmel and the routing of the priests of Baal, the three-and-one-half year drought did not end immediately. Elijah and a young man climbed to the top of Mount Carmel, 1,810 feet, to see if the rain was on its way.

"Go up now, and look to the sea," Elijah said to the young man. But nowhere could he see what Elijah wanted. "There is nothing," he reported. "Go again . . . go seven times." Elijah kept praying while the young man kept looking. Finally, on the seventh look, he came rushing back, excitedly exclaiming, "There is a cloud no bigger than a man's hand."

In a little while that cloud expanded until it covered the heavens; the wind came sweeping in from the sea, and there was "the sound of the abundance of rain."

We don't know much about drought here in my New Orleans—not with our average of sixty inches of rain per year. But having grown up in Oklahoma and the plains of West Texas, I know the joy that comes to people when, after a long dry spell, they hear "the sound"—not of a gully-washer, but of the gentle rain that soaks into the parched earth and gives it life.

You see, even after we decide about God, all of our problems are not solved immediately. It takes awhile for the rain to come. Then, evil never takes defeat lying down. Jezebel, in a rage, took out after Elijah. She would have his hide! But the "cloud" is the promise.

On the horizons of our dismal moral drought there are "clouds no bigger than a man's hand." As the TV commercial for Religion In American Life says: "Show Your Faith . . . It Can Shape the World."

This "cloud" idea calls for a full sermon. But briefly, see some of the "clouds" on our horizon.

The Indo-China war has been concluded. There is still fighting there, and we still have dreads and fears.

The Arabs and Israelis are at last coming to the negotiation table. We are giving more attention to the poverty problem in general, welfare reform, and the like. There are some serious efforts to get at pollution, ecology, and population control.

Violence and riots seem to be on the way out. In the racial area, no other nation in the world has ever tackled its racial problems in the head-on manner of the United States. Of course, we have a long way to go, but, my soul! What progress! Too slow and too little? Maybe so, from some viewpoints. Nevertheless, rapid and great from other viewpoints. More and better progress in human relations are inevitable.

Religiously, there is no great return to church. Maybe the various youth movements are portents. In our own church, we have more under 30's in attendance than over. It is our adult members who have habitually absented themselves from church across the years.

Clouds no bigger than a man's hand? Yes, but *clouds,* and clouds speak of the abundance of rain.

I want Mount Carmel to stand as a constant reminder that I must make up my mind who is to be God. So must you. As for me: "The Lord, he is God. . . I will serve him."

NOTES

1. *The Baptist Hymnal,* Hymn No. 418.

CHAPTER SIX

MOUNT HERMON—A COVENANT WITH GOD

DEUTERONOMY 4:44–49; 5:3; MATTHEW 16:13–20

"Not with our fathers did the Lord make this covenant, but with us, who are all of us here alive this day" (Deuteronomy 5:3)

Mount Hermon, sometimes referred to as Mount Zion, is known in the Bible as a "sacred mountain." Majestic Mount Hermon constitutes the northern limit of Israel's conquest. Rising 9,101 feet above sea level, it resembles an immense truncated cone, divided into three summits. Driving from Beirut to Damascus today one can get a lovely view of this mountain. From the top, there is a panoramic view of Lebanon, Damascus, Tyre, Mount Carmel, the mountains of upper Galilee, and the Jordan River to the Dead Sea. Hermon is covered with snow the year around. From the Dead Sea, 120 miles distant, its cool heights can be seen on torrid days. Its snowy whiteness is often reflected in the Sea of Galilee, and its melting snows are the main source of the Jordan River. Thus it is understandable why it figures in Hebrew poetry as the inspirational "high point."

By many, Mount Hermon is regarded as the "high mountain" referred to by Matthew, Mark, and Luke.

The nearness to Caesarea Philippi is an argument for its being the site of Jesus' transfiguration (Matthew 16:13). Such phrases in the transfiguration story as: "white as the light" (Matthew 17:2) "intensely white, as no fuller on earth could bleach them" (Mark 9:3) "dazzling white" (Luke 9:29) are reflections of the Mount Hermon setting. And the 133rd Psalm has a beautiful reference: "It is like the dew of Hermon, which falls on the mountains of Zion! For there the Lord commanded the blessing, life for evermore" (Psalm 133:3).

The heavy dews of Hermon are proverbial. Dew is nature's compensation for her failure to give rain and symbolizes refreshment and quickening, that is, new life and new energy. Palestine was desolate as a desert, until the people came together in the covenant fellowship. Then, like the dews of Hermon, freshness and life were brought along with the resurrection of the ideals of God. The reference in the Psalm is probably a reminder of the scene in Deuteronomy where Israel's *responsibility* under the covenant is stressed.

Since Israel had actually entered into a compact with God on Mount Sinai to keep his Law, there now comes a further sanction for obedience to that Law, an appeal to the will.

"Not with our fathers did the Lord make this covenant, but with us, who are all of us here alive this day" (Deuteronomy 5:3).

You see, this is no secondhand obligation. No covenant with God can ever be anything other than a *personal, firsthand agreement.* Faith in God does not come from inheritance, but from experience. Just as each new generation faces new tasks, so each generation must make its own covenant with God.

Some years ago on a train standing in line waiting to get into the dining car, I overheard part of a conversation. A man was talking, and said: "That man told me that he was *born* a Christian! That his mother and father were Christian, that their home was Christian, and he had never known when he was not a Christian." Keep this sentence in mind as you listen to a scene from Scholem Asch's novel, *Three Cities*.

Markin, desperately seeking to find himself after experiencing many sorrows and frustrations, came at last to Warsaw. He had broken his engagement to the lovely Nina, renounced his inheritance, and left his home in Petersburg. As he sat in the Hunting Home relating what had happened and expressing the desire to know and practice more effectively the faith of his fathers, he was interrupted by a teacher who said: "There can be no inherited faith. What we call faith must spring from our own experience . . . . Every one of us has found his own religion for himself, and has not merely taken it over from others."

These two episodes—the conversation on the train and the scene in the book—constitute the wide gamut of thinking concerning the matter of religious faith. While it may be true that we can be born into a Christian home, that does not make *us* Christian. If that were possible, then the physical and spiritual births spoken of by Jesus in his conversation with Nicodemus would be synonymous. And they are not.

About 150 years ago, Horace Bushnell of Yale advanced the idea in a book called *Christian Nurture* that children should be so reared they would never know themselves as being other than Christian. There is much in Bushnell's idea with which to agree, for that should be the responsibility of every Christian parent. However, many who follow Bushnell forget that he urged his own daughter to make a personal decision on the basis of her own Christian experience.

Faith is Personal

Faith, in its broadest sense, may be an inheritance. But it has little or no value until it becomes a part of our own experience. There are many varieties of religious experience, as William James pointed out. And no one can say that each must have the same experience. We can say that each must have an experience of his own. The experience of Peter was different from that of Paul. Yet each had inherited a certain amount of faith about a promised Messiah. Jesus of Nazareth became that Messiah for Peter and Paul when they entered into a covenant with him. Whether one's faith is mystical or practical, intellectually reasoned out or based on simple trust, it must be personal: "Not with our fathers, but with us."

In his *Spiritual Exercises*, intended for the training of Jesuits, Ignatius Loyola says that: "We ought always be ready to believe that what seems to us white is black, if the hierarchical Church defines it."

Now, that may be all right, if a person is willing to put blinders on his eyes and trust himself to the absolute guidance of another. In so doing he can have a kind of assurance that any such external authority provides. And it is a lot easier that way—to let someone else do your thinking and make your decisions. In my opinion, that is the major reason for the statistical success of Roman Catholicism and fundamentalist Protestantism. Each is a kind of handed down inherited faith which a person accepts.

But when any one of us will not accept his beliefs from someone else's say-so, the only way left for confidence in religious faith is to have a personal, inwardly convincing awareness of God that makes God indubitably real "not to our fathers, but to us."

To you, the reader, I would say:

I want you to be genuinely Christian. But I would not demand that you believe about Christ what I believe. What I see in Jesus Christ is not the question. The question is: *what do you see in Christ?* Surely, you cannot say that you see nothing to challenge your conscience, rebuke your life, or call for your commitment. Well, start with that, follow it as far as possible, then go on to see if there is anything more. This is not the time for objections to inherited creeds that have been meaningful to others, but whose ideas you cannot accept. I'm not asking you to believe all those ancient creeds. I am asking you to start where you are and follow what you do see and believe about God and Christ.

If Jesus himself saw you perceiving no more than you do right now, but wanting to try the adventure of following him, I believe he would encourage you by saying: "Don't bother about all you hear concerning me; start where you are." When he was on earth, all he said was, "Follow me." Only once did he ask, "Who do you say that I am?" Even in that dismal hour after Peter's denial, all Jesus said was: "Do you love me? Feed my sheep." Jesus did not get the full answer he desired about the quality of Peter's love. But Jesus did take the meager quality of Peter's love and went on with him from there.

Some years ago a noted biologist wrote a book entitled *Science and Religion,* in which he left the door wide open to the possibility of intelligent Christian faith. Another scientist reviewed the book. He was vexed that anyone should even desire religious faith and waste time on it. The reviewer had gone past discussing the credibility of religion and was skeptical of its desirability. Why, he wanted to know, should anybody *want* to believe in God?

Such an attitude is very much alive today, as it has always been, and is all too typical of certain limited areas of thought in our generation. It illustrates a disastrous separation that has taken place between religion and daily life.

That is the issue Moses was facing there on Mount Hermon. When a generation such as ours, or his, doubts the usefulness, desirability, and practical need of religion, then the church had better engage in some serious self-examination. And it is. It always has.

Something is happening to cause us to examine our faith in a new light. In order to show that such self-examination is no new thing, not only can we point to Moses, Joshua, Elijah, Jeremiah, and the New Testament, but look at something that was written almost a half century ago. Listen and see how very contemporary it sounds. The time of the writing is ten years after World War I, four years after an economic recession, and during an economic inflation prior to the stock market crash of 1929. Speaking of something calamitous happening to the meaning of religious faith, Harry Emerson Fosdick wrote:

It is indicated not so much in learned review and university lectures as in popular attitudes. The wide-spread neglect of institutional religion, the patent endeavors of multitudes of people, unconscious of any serious loss, to get

on without any religion at all, the wistful sense of spiritual
vacancy wanting to be filled but last of all thinking of a
church as the place to fill it, the idealistic movements . . .
whose associations with religion are remote and tenuous if
they exist at all—these and other elements in the present
situation bear witness to a crucial fact: contemporary human life, on the one side, and contemporary religion, on
the other, have been drifting apart.[1]

Many of us today feel that this same kind of mood is
making for much of the present turmoil in our churches.
Restlessness, especially among youth, and complacency
among older folk, is making a lot of people unhappy
about religious faith. Would this describe us?

Conscious of possessing spiritual good necessary to man's
fullest life, they are baffled by inherited forms of thought
and institution which have lost touch with the vital interests and habitual thinking of the people. Feeling thus out
of joint with their own time, some accuse the new generation of being sons of Belial, some urge the reformation of
the church, some blame education and cry out against the
colleges, some bewail the disturbance of old doctrines which
used to function as vehicles of the spirit and, presumably,
should do so still, some invent new religions to slake a
thirst which nothing but religion satisfies, and in general
the painful symptoms of impending change affect the house
of God.[2]

My soul, but that sounds contemporary. Even the
vocabulary is ours. But it was written in 1926. Again I
say, as each new generation has its own set of problems,
so each new generation must have its own personal
covenant with God. "Not with our fathers, but with
us."

On Mount Sinai we saw the original covenant with
God—a covenant of law. Here on Mount Hermon,
Moses, in his farewell address, shows that law, as such,
is not enough. It is not until Jeremiah, and most fully
in Jesus, that we see the inward personal quality of the
covenant.

The price of civilization is that life becomes complex, and the more complicated it becomes, the more
laws are needed to regulate it. Our legislatures—and
Congress—act under the apparent assumption that the
springs of righteousness in a community are not inward
but governmental, not spiritual but externally regu-
lative, and the assumption is bringing poor results. But
just because we must have laws, and unhappily must
have more of them the more complicated our life
becomes, all the more we need to guard ourselves
against depending on law for the safety and progress
of society. Whoever first said "you can't legislate
morals" was right. And an early mayor of New Orleans
was also right when he said, "You can make it illegal,
but you can't make it unpopular." (Martin Behrman)

Who can have lived during these last few years, with laws
piled on laws, governing every aspect of man's life, while
all the time lawlessness grows more rampant underneath,
without perceiving that not law but moral autonomy—the
desire and capacity of the individual citizen to govern himself from within—is the real underpinning of the state and
that, lacking this, the whole superstructure of legalism may
yet come clattering in ruin about our ears? [3]

Fosdick said that, too, in 1926. I believe this is what
Moses was trying to impress upon the children of
Israel some thirty-three centuries ago.

A covenant with God must always be contemporary, and it has to be personal. Some scholars indicate that the passage in Deuteronomy is a service of "covenant renewal." That is, a liturgical practice in which the covenant with God was renewed in each generation, so that each generation identifies itself with the original group at Sinai. This is one reason why we close each service of worship by asking that we *reaffirm* our faith.

To me, the necessity of a personal covenant comes most strikingly in the episode at Caesarea Philippi, recorded in Matthew 16:13–20, where Jesus asked, "Who do men say that the Son of man is?"

Many opinions were offered as an answer. But Jesus brings the question to a sharply personal focus: "But who do *you* say that I am?"

Call him Jesus of Nazareth, as history does,

"Son of the living God," as Peter did,

"Very God of very God," as the ancient creed did,

"The Man for all seasons," as many contemporaries do.

Call him what you will. Jesus Christ is so searching a fact that sooner or later each of us must make his own decision about a personal covenant.

So, I want Mount Hermon to remind us that a person must live by some faith. That we cannot escape. Some try to live by an inherited faith, which is custom, not faith. Some merely mirror the vague faith, or unfaith, of the society in which they live. But choice is given to us, a choice we cannot escape. Jesus Christ stands over against our world asking us, "Who do you say that I am?" And in that question there is the echo of Moses on Mount Hermon, saying, "Not with our fathers did the Lord make this covenant, but with us, who are all of us here alive this day."

NOTES

1. Harry Emerson Fosdick, *Adventurous Religion*, Grosset and Dunlap, p 16.
2. op cit, p 17.
3. op cit, p 17.

CHAPTER SEVEN

MOUNT ARARAT—A UNILATERAL PROMISE OF GOD

GENESIS 9:8–17

*"I set my bow in the cloud, and it shall be
a sign of the covenant between me and the
earth" (Genesis 9:13)*

Of all the stories in the Bible none is more familiar than the one about Noah and the flood. There is something timeless about this story that makes it popular. Bill Cosby's monologue about Noah is a best-selling record. A recent play on Broadway, *Two By Two,* starring Danny Kaye, is a retelling of the story of Noah. Orson Welles has one of the most poignant and dramatic scenes to be seen. In the role of an old Jewish rabbi, Mr. Welles tells the story of Noah.

For those who think Noah is nothing but a myth, there is the reminder that almost every record of ancient people has some reference to a great flood. The most forceful, other than the one in the Bible, comes from the Babylonian record. Something must have happened long ago, else these ancient historical records would not have mentioned it.

It is fitting that the first mountain mentioned in the Bible should be the highest of the biblical mountains. Ararat is a section of East Armenia, west of the Araxes

River, and today belongs to Turkey. Mount Ararat is a twin-peaked, majestic mountain rising 16,873 feet above sea level. It is almost equidistant from the Persian Gulf and the Mediterranean, Black, and Caspian Seas. It is named in Genesis 8:4 as the resting place of Noah's ark. Legends still persist that the remains of the ark are still there, and expeditions regularly search the area hoping to find that ark.

Forever Mount Ararat will be associated with the name of Noah, with God's great act of judgment, and God's unilateral promise not to destroy mankind again. As Mount Ararat rises above all the mountains of the Bible, so, standing upon its summit, we can survey the whole panorama of the divine revelation which reached its climax in Jesus Christ. We can learn two basic truths:

1. God is a God of righteousness, and punishment will follow sin.

2. God is a God of goodness and mercy.

The Flood

As previously stated, the story of Noah, the Flood, and the Ark are so well known that there is no need for a retelling of the story at this point. However, before getting into the main thrust of the unilateral promise of God, there are several things that deserve a brief comment.

For one thing, that powerful little sentence: "But God remembered Noah" (Genesis 8:1). The story of the flood does not end on a note of hopelessness. It may not seem of much significance when the dove came back with "one leaf," but it meant a lot to Noah. Remember that "cloud no bigger than a man's hand" that Elijah's servant saw? Noah could not eat that leaf, nor do anything with it that was useful, but it made the whole world *look* differently. It was a sign that out of the death and destruction new life was emerging.

Second, there is the Rainbow Covenant, which we merely introduce here, for this is to be our major theme later on. At the end of the catastrophe, a rainbow shines in the sky. The covenant with Noah is not a mutual agreement with mutual obligations. *It is a unilateral promise of God . . .* never to flood and destroy the earth again. And there are no conditions attached. The rainbow is a reminder to God of his obligation.

The Hebrew word for "bow" is always used to denote a weapon, and it goes back to the primitive idea that the lightnings are God's arrows, shot from his bow. Now, however, the lightnings are no longer arrows. The bow is put aside; the string is loosed—tied around God's finger to remind Him of his promise.

So what, if there had been rainbows before. So what, if the laws of refraction and reflection of light could explain the rainbow. This was something different.

The time comes when there is a definite need for a rainbow. In our own day, having faced two world wars, a world depression, and every other imaginable crisis, our civilization has passed through situations as dreadful, almost, as that flood. There are black memories and present fears of clouds that hang in the sky. If there is any rainbow, people don't see it. It is only when people see a rainbow, or something like it, that they can, like Noah, take up life again. The verb "to hope" is defined as "to cherish a desire with expectations."

In the thought of Israel, the flood brought vast destruction. But after the flood, *the rainbow*. After the tragedy, the great hope of a good future. The rainbow stands for the hope which tragedy cannot destroy. The rainbow which appears at the beginning of man's second chance also appears at the end: "and round the throne was a rainbow." (Revelation 4:3) The throne of God, which is beyond the human sky, has a rainbow around it. Here glorious expectation reigns. It means the fruition of everything that is good and beautiful. When he sees a rainbow around the throne of God, man comes to have a rainbow in his own mind.

A third thing to note is: "Noah became drunk" (Genesis 9:21).

Drunkenness is as old as history, and as unpredictable. Noah was a good man, but as the blunt truth of the Bible puts it, *he got drunk!* Maybe he got drunk on earlier occasions; we don't know. In that delightful drama, *Green Pastures,* Noah pleads with the Lord to be allowed to take some whiskey on board, just in case of snake bite. And snakes were on board, remember. He wants two kegs, one on each side of the ark for balance. The Lord finally allows him to take one keg— placed in the middle for balance.

Why did Noah get drunk, especially after the rainbow covenant? There are two possible reasons:
1. To escape from what he remembered about that dreadful experience.
2. To escape from the responsibility of what he had to do.
Escape from the past and the future—each is a cause to get drunk. Individual drunkenness is bad enough, but the drunkenness of society is worse—a drunkenness

caused by the heady wine of prosperity, or the new wine of power, or the old wine of idle optimism.

So we come to a fourth factor. According to the story, it was upon Noah and his family that the continuation of life on earth depended. Everyone else was gone. The second mankind was launched on its new life. One of the great themes of the Bible is "the saving significance of the remnant." That is, a small group is given the responsibility of going on with God's work.

The ark has become a symbol of the Church as that remnant. William Warburton, Bishop of Gloucester in 18th century England, wrote to a friend on June 13, 1751:

The church, like the ark of Noah, is worth saving; not for the sake of unclean beasts and vermin that almost filled it, and probably made most noise and clamour in it, but for the little corner of rationality, that was as much distressed by the stink within, as by the tempest without.[1]

Taking a seven-league-boot stride to the New Testament, we see the writer of Hebrews speaking about a "better covenant." And we ask, why better? Did God deliberately hold back something of himself? Was God over-severe in his judgment or deficient in his mercy? Why are these new promises better than the old ones? Could the writer mean that the new covenant brought forgiveness? So did the old. One thing is clear; there can be no grace of God without an honest confronting of the fact of our sin. The gospel of God's grace falls on deaf ears, unless men are ready to hear it. The "better covenant" is recorded in Hebrews 8:10: "I will put my laws into their mind, and write them on their hearts, and I will be their God, and they shall be my people."

But that was to Jeremiah. The *better,* the fulfilment, comes in Jesus Christ. Says Paul: "All the promises of God find their Yes in him" (II Corinthians 1:20) .

Now, let's get to the main thrust of the Flood story— *the unilateral promise of God.* (Unilateral means a contract arranged by and binding on only one party.) On his own initiative God says that he will not flood and destroy the earth again. So far as I recall, this is the only promise of God that is without condition on our part. Now it is up to us to bring the world and its people together instead of tearing apart. If the world and its people are destroyed again, *man will do it,* not God. And it seems that we are hell-bent toward our own destruction *unless . . .* !

There is risk, of course, in any unilateral action. Sometimes there is risk in a contractual agreement, a covenant, or a treaty that has obligations on both sides. Unless there is integrity, any agreement can be broken.

Right now we're hearing a lot about unilateral action on a military basis. Egypt wants Israel to unilaterally pull out of Sinai and other territories occupied since June 1967 with no obligation on Egypt's part. North Vietnam wants the United States to unilaterally withdraw from South Vietnam with no obligation on her part. Who knows for sure what would happen in either case? There are some who think that it just might be worth the risk.

In the third verse of the twenty-first Psalm is a phrase: "For thou dost meet him with goodly blessings." The King James Version says: "For thou *preventest* him with the blessing of goodness." The word "prevent" was already out-of-date in 1611, when the King James Version was published. More expert use of the Hebrew language, as well as a better use of modern English, has up-dated the word for our understanding, so we are told that God is one who "comes to meet us." That is, God is so far ahead of us that he has time to stop, turn around, and come back to meet us. This is an attribute of God which we seem to have not only neglected, but have forgotten altogether, if we ever knew about it. And this sovereignty of God is one of the most needed emphases of our day.

A.J. Gossip, the great Scottish preacher of a past generation, tells of hearing a man preach on the text: "Ask and it shall be given you." The preacher began by saying that God never gives unless we ask. This was an assertion, said Gossip, ". . .so entirely, obviously, and incredibly untrue that I never recovered." God never gives unless we ask? Why, 90% of what God showers upon us we have never asked for. Noah did not ask God for the rainbow. We never went running after God for the primary things which make life what it is. God came to meet us with what he had done in advance . . . from Creation on.

Very briefly, a reminder of some unilateral actions of God.

Ignatius Loyola sat down one day to make an inventory of the gifts God had given him for which he had never asked. He never got beyond the first item— *myself*. There he sat for hours staring at that one word, "I am a gift of God for which I never asked."

Every child has at some time asked, and every parent remembers the asking: "Why am I . . . *me?* Whenever we ask that question, either in childish naivete, or in adult sophistication, we become philosophers, puzzling over the meaning of life and our place in that life.

Whenever we make any kind of a place for God, at that point we become theologians.

Maybe this is a bit too abstruse for some of us; so let's look at it in a little more down-to-earth manner. If ours was the right kind of home, the advance gift to us was a home where we were wanted, where advance preparation was made for us to care for our every need.

Before our eyes could focus or our hands could hold or before we could utter a cry, provision was made for us. Before we could feel cold, we were wrapped in warm clothing. Before we could express hunger, there was mother's breast or a bottle of formula. You see, we came into a whole circle of advance, unilateral planning because there was concerned love.

Someone may say that this is just preacher talk, that this is love and care of human parents and has nothing to do with God. Of course, this is parental love. But it has a lot to do with God. If we take the Christian view of life as taught by Jesus, that God is the heavenly father, then parental love and provision is seen as an echo of the love of the heavenly father.

The same thing is true about the experience of salvation. Here, too, God surprises us in advance with a unilateral action. Salvation is nothing *we do*. Even when we respond to the call for repentance, it is because God took the initiative in the advance provision of Jesus Christ. The plan of salvation was in effect long before we ever came on the scene. And it is in effect whether we do anything about it or not.

Often at baptismal services we sing: "O happy day, that fixed *my* choice on Thee," as if we do the choosing and God is the object of our choice. To an extent, this

is true. But read again the story of the conversion of
Saul of Tarsus, for example. Looking back on the
strange events of the Damascus Road, he didn't know
what happened. He had not chosen Jesus; Christ had
chosen him. What took place there caused Paul bewilderment to the end of his days: "Unto me who am less
than the least of all saints, is this grace given" (Ephesians
3:8) he cried. You see, we don't have to go running
after God; he comes to us. In this greatest of all gifts,
God surprises us in advance.

This is the picture of God that we see throughout the
Bible—this surprising God who goes in advance, asking
for a covenant at one point, but making a unilateral
promise at another. Let's try and see the tremendous
implications this has for our whole Christian life.

For one thing, it means that when we are about God's
business, we do not have to try and drag God along with
us. We are in it in the first place because God has drawn
us there. This means that we have nothing to fear with
regard to hindrances that may come our way. If God is
as the Psalmist says he is, we will find him already
dealing with the obstacles.

For example, look at the little group of women who
wanted to do a last service for the master. Jesus had
been crucified and buried. So they started out early one
morning to anoint the dead body with the appropriate
burial spices. Then, a startling thing—the tomb was
sealed with a stone. So the melancholy cry, "The stone!
Who will roll away the stone?" And if you've never
heard an Arabic wail, you've never heard a cacophonous
sound. It goes on and on in the weird Oriental tonal
quality. Not even a mod-rock group, with all their

electronic amplification, has anything on an Arabic wail.

But note—they did not stop and hold an emergency prayer meeting. *They went on!* When they got right up to the tomb, they found the stone *already* rolled away. God surprised them in advance. *He got there first!*

The first thing they heard about the risen Christ was, "He is going before you into Galilee" (Matthew 28:7). Jesus had already said this to the disciples: "After I am raised up, I will go before you to Galilee" (Matthew 26: 32). And this he has been doing ever since—going before us into the common, everyday places of Galilee. What a challenge this is for us today!

The Church in Trouble

Ours is a day fearful for the future of the church. Indeed, there is fear for the total future of the Christian movement. The most convinced among us wonder just what the future holds for the Christian faith. Things are not too bright right now in the world, or at home, where Christianity is concerned. We wonder what will happen.

But, let us not feel that God has left us alone. God is already out there ahead of us. Somehow, the Holy Spirit is at work, as the wind blowing, although we do not see it. There is a dove with a leaf, a small cloud, and a remnant. Let us, therefore, ask: "What does it mean to follow Jesus out into this late 20th century Galilee of ours?"

To follow Jesus into Galilee brings us into sharp conflict with the forces of evil. The easy, surface peace of life is broken up into danger and difficulty. To be his follower demands an erect posture of ethical living, much harder to maintain than to sink back into an easy, careless moral slump, a sort of unconcerned lounging.

To follow Jesus into Galilee means the choice of "intangibles" instead of tangibles—faith, hope, and love instead of prestige, money, and comfort. To follow Jesus into Galilee puts us out of step with the passing parade. Jesus is an "irregular." If we try to follow him, we get out of step with the crowd. I remember during one of the early racial crises in our state, a prominent Baptist preacher said: "Jesus was a middle-of-the-roader." To which Dr. Frank Stagg, then professor of New Testament at the New Orleans Baptist Theological Seminary, replied: "Yes, Jesus was in the middle of the road. The thing is, Jesus was going in one direction, while everyone else was going in the opposite way."

Yes, the church today is in trouble, serious trouble. But the church belies all human evaluation, all human prognosis. G. K. Chesterton once said that Christianity has many times gone to the dogs, but in each case it has been the dog that has died. The church has many times appeared to have dwindled to nothing, and has then come alive again because God was in advance, waiting with a surprise. Let us never count God out! For God goes ahead of us and waits for us with the blessings of his goodness.

The Noah story ends with him and his family on dry ground, starting out with a chance to do with life on earth what Adam and Eve had a chance to do. *And Noah got drunk!* But there is that rainbow, tied around the finger of God as a reminder that whatever future destruction may come will come from man, *not from*

God! But a long time after Noah, when the centuries
saw man hell-bent toward destruction, God did something else—unilaterally—he sent Jesus Christ into the
world to allow us to see what life at its best really could
be.

I want Mount Ararat, with that rainbow tied around
the finger of God, to remind me of this surprising God
who goes in advance with a unilateral promise. But I
also want to walk down the middle of life's road, going
in the same direction as Jesus of Nazareth.

NOTES

1. The Interpreter's Bible, Vol. 1, p. 543.

CHAPTER EIGHT

MOUNT TABOR—FACING UP TO LIFE WITH GOD

JUDGES 4:4–9

*"The Lord, the God of Israel, commands
you, 'Go, gather your men at Mt. Tabor...'
... If you will go with me, I will go...."*
(Judges 4:6,8)

Five miles east and south of Nazareth, and twelve miles northwest of the village of Megiddo, Mount Tabor rises 1,929 feet abruptly out of the northern end of the plain of Esdraelon on the opposite side of the Valley of Jezreel. Standing on the summit, one can see to the north snow-crowned Mount Hermon and the peaks of Lebanon. To the northwest is the Sea of Galilee, and westward stretches the plains of Esdraelon.

Esdraelon is a fertile valley. Driving from Haifa, Israel toward Galilee, the modern tourist is impressed with the peaceful beauty and abundant crops. However, the tourist shudders as he realizes that this peaceful green valley has been irrigated with more human blood and fertilized with more bones of slain warriors than any comparable place on earth, including Gettysburg, Flanders Field, Anzio Beach, or even Vietnam.

From the earliest ages to the present, hostile armies have fought on those plains. Whether the modern tourist believes in a literal Armageddon that will be the last great battle of the ages or not, he knows what has happened here, and an involuntary shiver shakes him as he realizes that it could happen again.

History of Tabor

Let's take a quick historical journey and see some of the battles that have taken place on this peaceful plain at the foot of Mount Tabor.

Deborah and Barak gathered the thousands of Naphtali and descended to Esdraelon to do battle with Sisera and the Canaanites on the banks of the Kishon River. Since this is the basic episode for our theme, we will come back later.

Gideon and his army of 300, with their lamps, pitchers, trumpets, and shouts put to rout the armies of the Midianites.

The good king of Judah, young Josiah, marched out to meet the army of Egypt under Pharaoh Necho, and was slain.

The armies of the Crusaders in the 12th century clashed with the troops of Islam.

In more modern times, Napoleon, having conquered Egypt, set out to march on Syria. If he could hold on to the Bay of Acre, near modern Haifa, he would have the key to Palestine and could march northward to take Constantinople (Istanbul), and maybe go on to become another Alexander the Great. Along with General Kleber, Napoleon routed the Turkish army and the gate to Damascus was open.

On those same plains in World War I, General Alleny and the British army conquered the Turks, and the 400-year-old Ottoman Empire was crushed.

No wonder, then, that Megiddo gave its name to that battle mentioned in the Revelation, where it is said that the false prophet will gather the kings of the whole world into a place called Armageddon, to the last great battle of the ages.

The fourth and fifth chapters of Judges give two accounts of the same event on Mount Tabor. First in prose, then in poetry, the story of Deborah and Barak is told.

Deborah, the Leader

Women often play unusual roles in the destiny of men and nations. It is a bit unusual to find a woman in the place of leadership in a primitive age, especially in a society so masculinely geared as that of the Hebrews. Perhaps Deborah could be said to be a prototype of today's Woman's Liberation Movement.

Deborah's talents must have been many and great. She was a charismatic personality and was the rallying center for Israel against the oppressor, as Joan of Arc was for France. Maybe it would be better to say that she was an early kind of Golda Meir.

Deborah was a "judge" in Israel, which was the top place of civil leadership before there was ever a king, and the spiritual leader before there were prophets. She certainly was not the domestic type, although she was married. Her husband's name was Lappidoth, which means "firebrand." This could indicate that there may have been some "fireworks" in that home of two dominant personalities. We don't know whether Lappidoth objected to the many interests of his wife outside the home or not. If he did, it didn't make any difference. Deborah was destined for the arena of public affairs and military exploits; so Lappidoth just had to learn to live with a career woman, like it or not.

Deborah's sense of justice, so strong and helpful in Israel's internal problems, was outraged by Israel's subjugation to the Canaanites. Deliverance was imperative. So she called upon a man named Barak, which means "lightning," to assemble and lead an army of liberation.

The reader can sense the primitive drive of this woman. The passion of her patriotism and the depth of her religious feeling were so fused, that with abandon she urged Barak on and stood with him. Some say that Barak was weak to let a woman lead him. Not so! People were superstitious in those days too. If Deborah was a prophetess of God, then Barak would follow her and wanted her along. In fact, Barak's faith and courage are implied by Deborah's trust in him and her willingness to accompany him. And, after all, she was the people's leader.

It is no wonder that the account in Judges 5 is known as "The Song of Deborah." Here is a woman who needs an emotional outlet and finds it in the leadership of her people in a fight for liberation. Reading the story, one gets the feeling of Deborah's will power in the effect of a series of hammer blows:

She sent and summoned Barak . . . and said to him, 'Does not the Lord, the God of Israel, command you, Go, gather your men at Mt. Tabor'? . . . and she said, 'I will surely go with you' . . . Then Deborah arose, and went with Barak to Kadesh   (Judges 4:6,9) .

This is a striking story of a man challenged to do his best by a woman's courage and dynamism. Brooks Hays has a delightful little story which illustrates Barak's success. He says: "Behind every successful man stands two women: a knowing wife, and a surprised mother-in-law."

Another woman plays a prominent part in this story. Her name is Jael. Her role was to do what Barak had been unable to do in battle—capture and kill Captain Sisera. This is an intensely tragic scene. A weary man stumbles in grateful exhaustion into the tent of a woman he takes to be a friend. Her generous hospitality is made more cordial by milk and a cover while he rested in sleep. But while Sisera was asleep, Jael took a hammer and drove a tent peg through his head.

Ruthless and deceitful? Yes. But remember, those were rough times. Really, almost as rough as our own time when human life is cheap and a "contract" can be arranged for one man to murder another for pay. We, too, have known our Mata Haris. All governments use women as deceitful bait in the undoing of a man. But such evil deeds of deceit cannot be defended. We can try to understand on the basis of a ruthless age, an intense concern for Israel's well-being, and an "all's right in war" attitude so that whatever contributed to that end was all right. And, remember, we do the same thing today.

Yet, even the ancient writers did not regard this act of Jael as being inspired by God. In the early Christian era, the writer of the epistle to the Hebrews compiled that great chapter on faith (chapter 11) and mentioned many of Israel's judges: Gideon, Barak, Samson, Jeptha.

But he carefully omitted mentioning those of deceit and
violence, leaving out Jael, and even Deborah.

You Must Decide

Confusion and uncertainty are nothing new. This is
true not only in the social and political realm, but also
in religion. One of the great hymns of the church,
"Lead, Kindly Light," came from the travail of a man
distracted over his religion. However, our generation—
call it the new science, the atomic age, the space age, or
whatever—has accentuated our modern bewilderment.
Religious opinions today are painfully and radically
upset. Face life with God? Who or what is God? Is
there really a God?

Multitudes of people do not know what to think or
do. The winds of doctrine are gusty and variable.
There was a time of comparatively unanimous opinion
in things religious, with a settled, prevailing, strong
wind that blew one way. But not now. In this congre-
gation, there must be many of us who when faced with
the basic matters of religious faith—God, Christ, the
Bible, sin, salvation, prayer—often ask ourselves in our
own secret thinking what our opinion is. And, on the
other hand, what are we to do about these opinions. Is
there any facing life with God on our part?

We can sometimes postpone answering what is our
opinion. Sometimes we can postpone doing anything.
But there comes a time when a decision is forced upon
us. Circumstances cause us to form an opinion and take
a course of action. Mount Tabor is that kind of an
experience.

What is our opinion about God? We may not be able

to answer that. We may dally around with an answer, trying first this idea and then that, and decide that it is desperately difficult to make up our minds, and lay the question down—undecided. That is a familiar experience, and the result is agnosticism—not dogmatic atheism, denial of God, but perhaps a reverent agnosticism that can't be sure. But we live, one way or the other, as if there were a God, or no God.

What is our opinion in the debate between the protagonists of monogamous marriage on the one side, and temporary liaisons and promiscuity on the other? We may try to face these opposing views with suspended judgment. But we do act. One way or the other we live. We either go back to the polygamous instinct, or else we are true to the finest thing that has evolved in the history of family relationships—the instinct of monogamy.

Of course, there are areas where opinions do not affect our living, where living does not force a decision about our opinions. As to which of the various theories about the atmosphere on Mars is true, we don't know. We don't have to know. We don't even have to guess. We don't have to make up our minds about that because it has nothing to do with our lives.

But there are some troublesome questions that perplex us and do call for decision. We make up our lives, one way or the other. Maybe it's like being in a small boat, going down a powerful river and debating whether to stop at a given point. There may be opposing considerations that an open mind ought to face. Continue, then, the debate as to whether or not to stop. In the meantime, the river does not wait the conclusion of the argument, and sooner or later, if the debate has not settled the question, the river will have conclusively settled it. And life is like that.

What we are getting at is that religion, God, Christ, faith, salvation—call it what you will—is a forced decision. Of course, many details about religion are not. Whether you will be a Baptist or a Presbyterian . . . we're not talking about that. (Queen Elizabeth II is an Anglican when she is in England and a Presbyterian when she is in Scotland.) But intimate, vital, personal religion—that is something else. Whether or not this universe is aimless or whether there is purpose at the heart of it, whether it all came from a fortuitous self-arrangement of atoms or whether life is sustained by a creator, whether Christ is a revelation of something deep at the heart of reality or merely a psychological spark struck off from some physical collisions, and whether the end of it all is a coffin and an ash heap or an open sepulcher and hope—we live one way or the other about these opinions.

First, let's take this matter of faith in God. In one sense God is not a matter of faith at all, but a matter of fact. The Bible never argues about God, but assumes the fact of God, asks us to look at that fact, do something about it, and live as if God *is*.

Some creative power is behind this universe, producing everything that is in it and driving it. It is not by faith, but by factual experience that we know something about this power. It is law-abiding and never slips its leash. This strange creative power is actually here. We see the consequences of its operation. So, in that sense, God is not so much something we believe as observe.

But when it comes to interpreting this creative

power, opinions differ. Some say that it is nothing but physical. Others say that it is nothing but a machine. Look at a giant printing press into which at one end goes raw paper and at the other end comes out a finished product, marked all over with the signs of thought, ideas, ideals, aspirations, purpose. That is physical machine power. So, the universe may be a machine—strange that it made itself—into which raw matter enters at one end and from the other automatically comes humanity with its art, its science, its religion. That might be. But not for me.

When we use any symbol, drawn from human experience, as a description of God, we do it with humility, recognizing that it is partial and inadequate. I remember in grammar school geography being taught to think of Italy as being like a boot, thrust out into the Mediterranean, and Greece was like a hand with fingers. I still think of them that way. And, on a map, Greece and Italy do look somewhat like a hand and a boot. But how little that says about Greece and Italy— their history, culture, art, and ideas. Far more inadequate than that are all our symbolic images of God. Nevertheless, behind our partial symbol there is God.

Our proposition is that we cannot be neutral on that point. We may suppose that on a matter like faith in God we can reserve a decision and remain neutral. But we cannot. We act and live one way or the other. We face life as if there were no God, or there is a God.

I am not trying to avoid the merely intellectual arguments about God. I must say, however, that on intellectual grounds (at least *my* intellectual grounds) the proposition that a number of physical particles fortuitously moving into an empty void could arrange themselves into planets, sunsets, human beings, music, art, poetry, science, astronauts—*Christ; that is too in- credible for me to believe.

The decision is between God and no-God, between an aimless and purposeful universe, and we can't escape it.

Come a step further and face life in reference to faith in man. Not only is God a matter of fact and faith; so is man. There are a lot of facts about man, most of which we know about. But what do we make of them? How do we interpret them? Is man, for example, merely a machine—as some claim—with some interesting mental and spiritual by-products? Maybe so, but that idea presents some serious difficulties.

We human beings may be driven from behind by combinations of heredity and environment, but we are also lured by ideas and ideals in front of us, enticed by goals and purposes we can choose. We even cry with Tennyson, ". . . Ah for the man to rise in me. That the man I am may cease to be." Imagine a machine doing that!

We human beings repent, sometimes with heart- breaking remorse, for wrongs done, and penitently seek pardon and make restitution. No machine ever did that! We human beings look up to something above and beyond us; however, we may describe the values we reverence. We sometimes even "love the highest when we see it" and give ourselves to it in selfless dedication. Picture a machine doing that!

When the materialist insists that we human beings are mere machines, while we grant that it is quite obvious that there is a mechanistic aspect to us all, at least they must acknowledge that we are machines that think, love, distinguish between right and wrong, repent, follow ideals, sacrifice for one another, believe in God, hope for immortality, and construct philosophies to explain the universe. Queer machines! Nevertheless, we might be, I suppose, some kind of physiochemical product. Or it might be, on the other hand, that the deeper truth lies in the ancient faith that, "We are children of God, and if children, then heirs, heirs of God, and fellow heirs with Christ" (Romans 8:17).

What we are saying is that we cannot face life by being neutral on the question of man. Sooner or later, assumptions do appear in life with reference to human value and destiny, on which we habitually act. Put over against each other two extreme views—the estimate of man that Jesus had, when he died for man because he thought man was worth dying for, and on the other side the skeptical estimate that says, "The cosmos is a gigantic fly-wheel making 10,000 revolutions . . . Man is a sick fly taking a dizzy ride on it." You see, this business of thinking about man is not simply a question of theory; it is a fundamental matter about how we face life.

In the third place, let's see that this same truth applies to faith in the future, about hope and hopelessness. It may be that death ends it all, that when we die, "that's all she wrote." Someone said it could be that:

This generation is a bonfire to warm the hands of the next generation and that that generation will be another bonfire to warm the hands of the next, and that in the end this whole human conflagration will burn itself out and end in an ash heap.

That might be. On the other hand, it could be that the creative power at the heart of all things being spiritual, the creative process called life cannot end on an ash heap, that every winter will have its spring—that every Good Friday will have its Easter morning. We cannot work out the argument on these two possibilities with absolute finality. And, because it is difficult to get an assured answer, some folk try to avoid making up their minds. But life does it anyway.

One scientist said that the greatest tragedy that had ever happened in the universe was the evolution of consciousness. That is, he lived in a universe so dark and damnable that the greatest tragedy was that human beings should develop consciousness to know just how dark and damnable it is. Such hopelessness is one way of living. But there is another way: "This corruptible must put on incorruption and this mortal put on immortality, and what eye has not seen nor ear heard, nor the heart of man conceived what God has prepared for those who love him" (I Corinthians 2:9). Or, as Morris Reynaud, our aged black church custodian, put it: "God breathed life into Adam, didn't he?; and that breath of God is never goin' away."

Well, we've gotten down off Mount Tabor and have wandered all over the plains of Esdraelon to do "jawbone" battle with some encamped Canaanites, and Sisera has escaped. It may seem that the detour has taken us far from the scene on Mount Tabor with which we began. Maybe it has. On the other hand, perhaps there is something in the episode of Deborah and Barak that fits into all of this.

As we've said, confusion and uncertainty are nothing new. That's what Deborah faced: life of confusion, uncertainty, fear, and frustration. But she faced life with faith in God, not just some idea about God, but faith in the fact of God, and her faith led her into action.

She faced life with faith in man—Barak and his army. If Barak was on the weak side, needing support, she believed in him and his fellows strongly enough to go along with them and confront the enemy who was causing the confusion.

She had faith in tomorrow. Maybe it was not a belief in immortality. But she believed tomorrow could be better than today. *It had to be!* And if it was to be better, something had to be done about Sisera and the Canaanites.

It may be that there are some whose lives are better than their creed. Ask them if they believe in God, man, and immortality, and they would say, "No." But they live as though they did. Would it not be better to find some belief, some faith, no matter how little, latch on to it, and live by it?

There are probably some folk whose lives are worse than their creed. With resounding declaration they say, "Of course we believe in God, in man as God's child, and immortality as life's goal." But they don't live as though they believe this. Would it not be better to add right living to right faith?

And, surely, there are some who say they just don't know, they just can't be certain. But they are living as though they do, or do not, believe. They can't avoid that.

So, I want Mount Tabor to remind us that whatever Siseras are causing our confusion, we can face life with faith in God, faith in man, and faith in tomorrow.

CHAPTER NINE

MOUNT OF TRANSFIGURATION—
FROM MOUNTAIN TO VALLEY

MARK 9:2–29

*"And after six days Jesus took with him
Peter and James and John, and let them
up to a high mountain apart by themselves; and he was transfigured before
them." (Mark 9:2)*

The concept of God that we have causes us
either to want to stay on mountains of pious meditation
or go into valleys of rugged service. We need both. We
cannot be activists all of the time, nor can we fold our
hands in meditation all of the time. There is a time for
each.

An ancient tradition, dating back to the time of
Jerome in the 4th century A.D., makes Mount Tabor
the scene of Jesus' transfiguration. However, other
traditions point to Mount Hermon as the place. Perhaps
a better case can be made for Mount Hermon, although
the actual place makes little difference. What happened
there is what is important. Remember, though, that
Hermon is one of the highest Palestinian mountains,
being 9,101 feet above sea level.

The time of the transfiguration was probably at
night. We read that Jesus was praying, and he usually
prayed at night. Also, the disciples were asleep—the
same three that later slept during the Gethsemane
prayer. After climbing the mountain they were tired;
they went to sleep. It was a perfectly natural thing to

do. While they slept, Jesus prayed, and "As he prayed, the fashion of his countenance was altered, and his raiment was white and glistening" (Mark 9:3).

As he was praying, Moses and Elijah appeared and spoke with him concerning his coming death in Jerusalem. In the midst of this conversation, the disciples awoke. Startled and thrilled by what they saw, Peter blurted out, "It is good for us to be here; let us make three tabernacles" (Mark 9:5). But they couldn't stay. They had to go back to the valley. In the valley they faced the demoniac lad, and they were helpless. Life cannot always be lived on mountaintop kinds of experiences, delightful and valuable as they are; there are always valleys of reality and need.

All three synoptic Gospels record this scene, but only Luke tells us that the transfiguration took place while Jesus was praying. It is characteristic of Luke to stress the importance of prayer to Jesus. He often speaks of Jesus' prayer life. Luke also tells us the subject of the prayer: ". . . his departure which he was to accomplish in Jerusalem" (Luke 9:31).

The prayer in Gethsemane, also in the sleeping presence of Peter, James, and John, dealt with this same theme. It is natural that death would preoccupy Jesus' mind. Was it really necessary for him to die? Was death God's will for him?

Whatever else we may say about the transfiguration, it is one of the most significant experiences of the New Testament. The Gospel writers look upon the incident as being divine confirmation of Jesus' messiahship.

It is hard to understand Peter's subsequent denial of Jesus in the light of this experience. And it is also hard to understand why the three kept silent about it, even if Jesus did tell them to. How did Matthew, Mark, and Luke learn about it, and when? No matter, something happened—either after the resurrection, as some scholars believe, or before, as we have it recorded.

There are several places in the story where we could stop and build tabernacles, as Peter wanted to do. "What are you discussing?" (Verse 11). "I asked your disciples to cast it out, but they were not able" (Verse 18). "All things are possible to him who believes" (Verse 23). "I believe; help my unbelief" (Verse 24). "This kind cannot be driven out by anything but prayer" (Verse 29).

Without really stopping, let's at least pause and take a quick tourist's look at several things before we get to the major idea I want to stress.

No wonder Peter wanted to stay there. It was a good experience, and we want to make good experiences permanent. But there is danger in a too easy satisfaction—*the danger of getting life pegged at some point*. This is what the psychologists call "halting the procession."

Often, when we confront the potentials of tomorrow, someone is tempted to say, "This is as far as I want to go," and life becomes fixed there. Instead of our moving on to new experiences and achievements, this one great achievement becomes the pivot around which we move.

In one of John Marquand's novels he has a character, Bojo Brown, who, no matter what the occasion or conversation, always manages to get in the fact that in his senior year at Harvard he scored the winning touchdown in the game against Yale. Bojo pegged life at that high spot. I have a friend, now in his mid-40s with a graduate degree, who still talks about his high school exploits as if life had stopped there.

It is tragic for anyone to block the progress of life's possibilities at any level. But it is a far worse tragedy for a person to move on everywhere and in everything else and leave his religious life pegged at some point in the past.

Sometimes this is because of a premature rejection of faith which throws the baby out with the bath. One may feel dissatisfied with youthful religious teaching, not pleased with what one now has, but unwilling to search for more, that life is chained to an inadequate spot and no genuine exploration of the Christian faith is attempted. A faith that is not allowed to grow is no longer capable of fitting into an expanding world of experience and need.

Someone else has an unfortunate experience in church, so he grows sour on the whole thing, blaming all other churches, and pegs his life outside the church, hurting mostly himself. A neighbor child who butchers Beethoven in his piano practice doesn't cause him to rule out all music, nor does a malpractice suit against a doctor keep him from seeking medical attention. Only in the church does he peg life at a sour point.

Think what Peter would have missed had he been allowed to stay on that mountain, saying, "Look how far we have come!" which would have caused him not to see how far they still had to go.

That little question of Jesus, "What are you discussing?" also deserves a pause. There is a sting in the word "discussing." In the presence of an emergency, all they could do was discuss—talk. The sad plight of an epileptic lad called for more than words. Our current *in* word is "dialogue," which means the same thing. How many times in human history have Jesus' disciples,

faced with appalling human need, been preoccupied
with words instead of deeds?

Ascending the Valley

Long years of religious wars, accompanied by discussion over fine points of heresy; the scourge of
slavery talked about for centuries, with few hands
lifted to free slaves; and so today valleys of human need
more talked about than acted upon. The major emphasis for us to see is "from mountain to valley."

The contrast between the scene on the mountain and
the episode in the valley is sharp. Instead of lonely
solitude, we have a large crowd; instead of Moses and
Elijah, we have a distraught father and an epileptic son;
instead of a reassuring voice from heaven, we have a
vocal complaint about the failure of the disciples. There
is also an implied contrast in the mood of Jesus.

Instead of conversing with God, Moses, and Elijah,
he is not only disturbed by the poignant case of human
need, but is also disappointed in the failure of the
disciples; instead of communing with God, now he must
confront what was called a demon.

However, these contrasting pictures stand together
as one scene. Jesus, the one whom God approved on the
mountain, is now the one through whom God acts in the
valley. Jesus' glory is not to be detached from human
beings, but is to be relevant to every human situation.

One of the finest expositions of this passage comes,
not from Bible scholars, but from an artist—Rafael's
great painting of the descent of Jesus from the Mount
of Transfiguration. Rafael shows powerfully the striking

contrast between the top of the mountain and the bottom.

Above, the beauty of that high vision; below, tragic need and suffering; above, the glorious conversation; below, the impotence of the disciples.

Life repeatedly shows the place of high spiritual privilege and close beside it the place of suffering and confusion. The tragedy is compounded because often the very people who have had the high vision and experience with God make no vital connection of that with the needs of their fellow men.

In one of George Moore's novels he tells of Irish laborers in the great depression. They were put to work by the Irish government on a make-work project to build roads. At first, the men worked well, sang their Irish songs, glad to be back at work again. Gradually, the men discovered that the roads they were building didn't go anywhere; they just ran off into the dreary bogs and stopped. As this truth dawned upon them, the men grew listless and stopped their singing. Their work quality slipped. Commenting, the author said: "The roads to nowhere are difficult to make. For a man to work well and sing, there must be an end in view." This is the same principle found in *The Bridge Over the River Kwai*.

Peter, James, and John could have stopped and stayed on that mountain, but they would soon have become bored, for it led to nowhere.

This terrifically complicated world situation of ours affects us all in varied ways. Sometimes we may feel that getting away from the hectic times in the valley to a mountain of meditation is what we need. And we do need that. But there is one effect everyone of us must feel. The mountain makes our ordinary tasks seem trivial.

Here is a stupendous upheaval, threatening to shake civilization to pieces, like a big dog shaking a little dog. This is the greatest revolution, we are told, since the downfall of the Roman Empire, or the Renaissance, or the Protestant Reformation. Yet, we go on, day after day, with our common duties, household tasks, office routines, professional services, helping a little here and there if we can. How trifling it all seems. But, why shouldn't we go on about our daily tasks in as normal a manner as possible? We can't resign from the human race, even if some are trying. We can't all be hermits, or live in so-called idyllic communes. We can't wash our hands of responsibility. Pilate taught us that.

To be sure, this feeling of the humdrum is a major curse of human life, even in what are called "normal times." And our time is anything but normal or ordinary. Because of this, many people die along the way before they are really dead, their lives lose zest, and a dull drab fog of complacency falls over them.

Maybe this is one reason for the restlessness of our youth; they don't want life to be ordinary; they will not have it so, for they will not build roads that lead to nowhere. My generation had to shake itself out of the dullness of that Great Depression, and other factors, with a feeling that we had to go somewhere. Today's youth is no different. One thing is at least clear—to have our commonplace living elevated, dignified, and made meaningful would be a redeeming experience.

One valley of today's ordinary life could be called "getting on with people." There are many ways of describing war and its causes, for example. But the gist of the matter is that people can't get on with each other. We can analyze racial prejudice, go through its historic background, and define its essential causes—Black/White, Arab/Israeli—but it boils down to people getting on with each other.

Despite all of our revulsion to war and racial prejudice, here we are saddled with them, for a reason that gets down into the valley, to the level places of ordinary life. People just find it hard to get on with one another.

Where, then, is the ground of our hope that sometime, even as great nations, we can learn to live with one another? Well, for one thing, that mountain experience with God is needed—an experience that convinces us that God is the Father of us all, no respecter of any, and has set up some guidelines for us to live by.

Then, that hope is grounded on the fact that in a thousand and one ordinary, day-by-day little experiences, good will does work; friendship is effective; tolerance and mutual understanding do compose differences; cooperation displaces hostility, and we do respect each other when we know each other.

Today we have German and Japanese friends; tomorrow we could have Russian and Chinese friends, too. I have both Arab and Israeli friends, and there are some limited friendships on both sides of that uneasy line. Despite "Yankee, go home!," the individual American is a welcome guest. We could feel at ease on the streets of Cairo, and would probably be a lot safer there than on the streets of New York, Washington, or even New Orleans.

A century and a half ago, two poets—Coleridge and Wordsworth—set themselves to a task. One was to declare "the commonplace of the wonderful," and the other described "the wonderful of the commonplace." These are not the terms they used. Rather, they spoke of the natural and the supernatural. We see this in this episode in the life of Jesus. The mountain is the supernatural, the wonderful; the valley is the natural, the commonplace.

There is an element in our American temperament which runs counter to the truth we are trying to obtain. We Americans have been notoriously impressed by size —big country, big business, big buildings, big churches, the biggest this or the biggest that. We are noted for our interest in bigness. To say of anyone that "he does things in a big way" is the highest of American compliments.

In the church realm, this is likewise our temperament. Bigness has been our criteria—the biggest denomination, the biggest church, largest Sunday school, largest budget, highest debt. Most, biggest, and largest are our descriptive nouns. Ours is a statistical syndrome with an edifice complex. Now that we have leveled off, begun some decline from the mountain, with statistics dropping, we are almost in a panic, not quite knowing what to do. We are finding it difficult to come off the mountain into the valley.

Other church groups, Protestant and Catholic, face the same thing. We have looked at ourselves from every angle. There has been self-study, self-criticism, self-flagellation. What are we to do? Using psychiatric language,

"A person can't stay in analysis forever. At some point a person has to get up off the couch and learn to live with himself as he is and with things as they are, and go on!"

The Church at Ephesus

Let's illustrate with a scene from the life of Paul and show that the Church at Ephesus is a good example of going into the valley. That there was a church at all in Ephesus is almost incredible. One of the most important cities of the Roman Empire, Ephesus was dominated by the worship of a fertility goddess named Diana. The city was fabulously wealthy and full of factions, rivalries, and jealousies.

Along came a "bald-headed little Jew," as Harry Golden describes Paul, saying: "I will stay in Ephesus until Pentecost, for a wide door for effective work has opened to me, and there are many adversaries" (I Corinthians 16:9).

About Paul, one can say that he had an aggressive personality. There is a temptation to use the word "offensive," but there is another connotation to that word. "Here in Ephesus I have found an open door," and as a kind of after thought, he added: "And there are many adversaries." That isn't the way most of us would think or act. Most of us would have listed the adversaries and as a kind of afterthought, he added: "And there are are opportunities.

There at that level place, at the foot of the mountain, the disciples saw the adversary, the difficulty—the demoniac boy—more than they saw an open door of opportunity.

If we were charged with evangelizing Ephesus, starting a church there, what would we do? Probably ask our "New Work Committee" to make a survey. And I'm all for that. We'd check the real estate market, the cost of building construction, the financial ability of interested families who would support a church, and what reaction we would get from the established religion and the public officials.

With the data in hand, we would hear a report something like this:

Whereas, there exist in Ephesus certain adversaries, and by reason of their hostility, a strong disinclination to support a new work at this time, therefore, be it resolved that we postpone consideration of the matter at this time. But be it further resolved that we be ready to establish a church at Ephesus when present hostility has subsided and circumstances are deemed more favorable to the situation. [1]

But to Paul, Ephesus was an open door. Ephesus, with not a Christian in it, with nothing there but strong winds of opposition. How could Paul do it? How could Dr. James Young do it, first in Gaza, and then in Yemen—the first Christian missionary ever in Yemen?

Well, he had resources. He had been to the mountain. Remember his conversion on the Damascus Road, and his fortification by days of meditation in the desert. Now he was ready for the valley. He knew what Jesus meant about "These kind do not come out except with fasting and prayer."

One year the Rockefeller Foundation Report on Education said:

What most people want, young and old, is not merely security or comfort or luxury, although they are glad enough to have these. Most of all, people want meaning in their lives—meaning, mission, and purpose.

George Moore was right. It's the roads that lead to nowhere that are hard to make and take. What takes the heart out of us is not the problems we face. We can tackle anything, stand almost anything, so long as we can believe that there is some meaning in what we are doing, and if we have had an experience that convinces us of our place in it all.

Our western civilization, especially the American version of it, has emphasized action. We have not yet developed a technique of meditation nor seen the real necessity of prayer. We are activists. Let's get the job done. And there is something very Christian about activism. Those disciples wanted action with that boy. Jesus was also an activist; he did something about that boy. I think action is preferable to the passive technique of the East where the Guru sits all day with hands folded in contemplation, unclasping them only long enough to strum his sitar, gaze at a flower, or accept alms. Someone has to support that Guru!

Still, we can't be activists all the time. Even football is not action all the time. There is that little "prayer meeting" called the huddle where the next play is called.

Activist that he was, Jesus knew the necessity of prayer beforehand. He knew there was a right combination of prayer and action, mountain and valley. We need that, too.

So, I want that Mountain of Transfiguration to remind me that I need his experiences with God, that I can't build an altar, peg life down, and stay there; I must get into life's valleys. But, I can't meet the valley situations unless I've found the inner resources of God.

NOTES

1. J. Wallace Hamilton, *Where Now Is Thy God?* p. 28

CHAPTER TEN

MOUNT OF OLIVES—COMMUNION WITH GOD

II SAMUEL 15:30; ACTS 1:12

"And when they had sung a hymn, they went out to the Mount of Olives." (Mark 14:26)

A mile-long ridge of rounded limestone hills roughly paralleling the eastern elevation of Jerusalem is called Olivet. Almost in the center of the ridge is the Mount of Olives, the most conspicuous landmark of Jerusalem. The mountain is separated from the plateau of the city by the deep, narrow cleft of the Kidron Valley. This mountain is "a Sabbath's day's journey from Jerusalem," a little more than half a mile.

The northernmost and highest point, 2,723 feet, in earlier times was called Viri Galilae, because many locate the ascension of Christ here. In more modern times, Hebrew university and a hospital were located. Both were closed and unused from 1948, when Jordan controlled the old section of Jerusalem. But since the "Six-Day War" of June 1967, Israel has reoccupied this area.

The next principle hill is 2,641 feet and is also called "the ascension" place. A Russian Orthodox Church is located here, with its tall Tower of Ascension. It can be seen from all approaches to Jerusalem. Nearby is a small Moslem chapel, also claimed to be the spot of Jesus' ascension. From this point can be seen an unsurpassed

119

view of Jerusalem. Maybe it was here that Jesus wept
over his beloved city.

The third elevation is called "The Prophets," because
tradition says that some of the Old Testament prophets
were buried there.

Fourth is the Mount of Offense, 2,411 feet, and is
so named because of Solomon's apostasies on this site.

On the lower levels of the Mount of Olives is the
Garden of Gethsemane. What was once a large area is
today a small, beautiful, well-kept garden and a few
old olive trees. It is now fenced in because of the van-
dalism of tourists wanting souvenirs. The garden is main-
tained by the Franciscan order of the Roman Catholic
Church. However, there is also an Armenian and Russian Orthodox section of the garden.

The Mount of Olives is mentioned only occasionally in the Old Testament. King David fled over it barefoot during Absalom's rebellion: "But David went up
the ascent of the Mount of Olives, weeping as he went,
barefoot and with his head covered . . . David came to
the summit, where God was worshipped" (II Samuel
15:30,32).

Evidently, there was some kind of a shrine already
there. We can see a kind of suggested comparison in the
sorrows of David here and the agony of Christ in the
same place. David was weeping over the rebellion of his
son, Absalom; Jesus' agony was over the sinful rebellion
of all men.

Ezekiel referred to the mountain on the east side of
the city, although he did not call it by name (11:23).
And Zechariah made the Mount of Olives God's van-
tage point for watching the powers that were threatening Jerusalem (14:4).

Before acquiring calendaric knowledge during the Babylonian Exile, Jewish religious leaders announced the coming of each new moon by signals lighted on the Mount of Olives after the Sanhedrin had observed its first slender crescent.

One thing we can say for certain—the Mount of Olives is one biblical spot about which there is no argument. However, there is considerable speculation about the specific places on that ridge where certain events occurred.

We know that the Mount of Olives was a favorite place for Jesus. It was his custom to go there at evening when other men went to their homes. From its top he could see his beloved city of Jerusalem. And almost every scene we have sees Jesus in prayer there.

Some say that it was on the slopes of the Mount of Olives that Jesus taught his model prayer to the disciples. At least we can get this impression from Luke's gospel (11:1–4). This event is memorialized by a chapel on whose walls is the Lord's Prayer written in thirty-five different languages. It is a moving spiritual experience to stand in that chapel, look at the prayer in those languages, and want to say: "O, for a thousand tongues!" But according to the sixth chapter of Matthew, the prayer was a part of the Sermon on the Mount, which took place in Galilee. Maybe there were two occasions when Jesus taught the prayer. One teaching on anything by anyone is seldom enough.

From the hilltop village of Bethpage Jesus rode a borrowed colt down the steep side, across the Kidron Valley, and up the bank to enter the walled city of Jerusalem through what was called the Golden Gate. We call this The Triumphal Entry of Jesus into Jeru-

salem, or Palm Sunday, because palm branches were
strewn along the way. Only John (12:13) describes the
branches as being palms, for palm trees do not grow in
this area of Palestine.

After observing the Passover with his disciples, the
occasion where he instituted the Last Supper in the
Upper Room, Jesus and the Eleven went to the Mount
of Olives. Those ancient olive groves in Gethsemane on the slope witnessed his agonizing appraisal
of himself and his task, his prayer, the betrayal by
Judas, and the arrest.

It would be easy to pick any one of the episodes and
say this is the event of significance on the Mount of
Olives. By all means, as significant as anything is the
prayer life of Jesus. And we will come to that. There
are two scenes that I want us to see—the Triumphal
Entry and the Garden of Gethsemane. These two events
are especially meaningful for Palm Sunday and Good
Friday.

As Jerusalem confronts Jesus that week before Easter,
one fact stands plainly out. What a relief it would have
been if they had not had to confront him! It is obvious
that the majority of the city did not want to accept him;
no majority ever does. Nor do I think that the majority
wanted to kill him. No majority wants violence; only
minorities operate that way. But the larynx of a minority mob can too often overcome the mind of the
majority. If only they could have dodged the issue
and done nothing about him, what a relief!

Who could come into our city and arouse the majority of us? Eldredge Cleaver woud get a few partisans
and more opponents, but most wouldn't care. Billy
Graham would draw maybe 40,000, but most wouldn't

care. Pope Paul VI would get more attention, but most would probably go on about their affairs. The President of the United States would perhaps draw the biggest crowd, but not the majority. Only King Rex of Mardis Gras can throw our entire city out of kilter. Most want to dodge issues.

Surely, this factor was present in Pilate, although, because of his position, he was thrust into a place where he could not steer clear of Jesus. He wished he could avoid the responsibility. Any acceptance of Jesus was preposterous, out of the question. Crucifying Jesus was distasteful, as well as having a martyr on his hands which could lead to real trouble. Not that Pilate was afraid of trouble, or didn't have the power to crush a rebellion. But trouble isn't good on the record of an administrator who wants to move up the ladder. Why did he have to have anything to do with Jesus? His wife had told him to have nothing to do with the man. He even symbolized his desire to side-step the issue by publicly washing his hands of the whole matter.

Let's recognize our kinship with Pilate in our instinctive desire to side-step issues. In some ways, we are all escapists, wanting to run away from decisions, and naturally so, because decision-making is the hardest work in the world. To be neither for or against anything, just neutral, that is the desire of most.

But alas! Life is not made for neutrals. Life habitually confronts us not with three choices, as most assume —pro, con, and neutral—but with *two* choices—pro and con, for or against, one or the other. And no place is this more true than when it comes to Jesus. When Jesus said "He that is not with me is against me" (Matthew 12:30). And "He that is not against us is for us" (Mark

9:40) He stated the kind of fact that forever defeats the
Pilates who try to wash their hands of some great matter.

In the psychological realm we face this fact. Habit,
for example—what a nuisance it is to have to choose
between habits. Sobriety or drunkenness, sexual self-
control or promiscuity, harnessed temper or explosive
anger, Christian altruism or self-centeredness—if one
could only be neutral about such matters. But, try as
we may to wash our hands, one way or the other we do
become creatures of habit. As the ancient Chinese prov-
erb says:

> Sow an act and reap a habit;
> Sow a habit and reap a character;
> Sow a character and reap a destiny.

We face this, too, on a broader scale. American isolation was once an effort toward neutrality. World War
II changed that and taught us that we cannot be isolated from the world. Since that time we have found
out, the hard way, just what a pesky nuisance international interdependence really is, and what bother-
some responsibilities go along with world leadership.
We might want to withdraw to within our two oceans
and two friendly neighbors and say, "The world be
damned!" But there is no way for us to do that . . .
not now, not with atomic fall-out coming to us from
Russia and Red China, and ours going over to them.

When Jesus left the Mount of Olives he "steadfastly
set his face to go to Jerusalem." We most often think of
what this meant to Jesus: *his death!* But let's think, too,
of what it meant to Jerusalem. If he had only stayed
away! Confronting Jesus, some welcomed him with

shouts of praise; others were equally convinced that he had to be gotten rid of.

Jesus Christ is disturbing. We Christians speak of his love and give him glorious names. While Jesus did speak of love, he also said that he came to cast fire upon the earth. To our human nature Jesus is upsetting. Why must we be haunted by his ideals so far above us, and made miserable by his demand of choosing either for or against him? Why can't he just let us alone? Would not life be easier if he had never come to bother us with his demands? But he did come! Palm Sunday reminds us that he comes from Olivet to our Jerusalem.

A great theologian of the last century, Soren Kirkegaard, whose influence has powerfully revived in our time because he so forthrightly tells the truth about us, said:

Let us collect all the New Testaments that are in existence, let us carry them out to an open place or up upon a mountain, and then, while we all kneel down, let someone address God in this fashion: Take this book back again; we men, such as we are now, are no good at dealing with a thing like this, it only makes us unhappy. My proposal is that like the inhabitants of Gadara we beseech Christ 'to depart out of our coasts'.

What we are talking about now is a personal fact. Whenever an individual faces Jesus, he faces a decision. That was what it was in the New Testament. That is the way it is now. I am asking now that we face Jesus as he confronted people and make a decision: Zacchaeus, with his dishonest exploitation; Dives, mishandling wealth, Mary Magdalene, misusing sex, the Pharisees, with their race prejudice, hating all Samaritans, Nicodemus, needing to be born again . . . these and others. We will find ourselves somewhere in one of them. And the question is: Will we or won't we?

Well, if it sounds harsh to say that we must confront this disturbing Christ, let's see another side of it.

The humanist scholar, Muretus, in the 17th century, a fugitive from France, fell ill in Lombardy, and, looking like a vagabond in rags, asked aid of some doctors. The physicians discussed his case in Latin, not thinking that this bedraggled wretch could understand the learned tongue of scholars. They said: "Let us try an experiment with this worthless creature." To their amazement, that worthless creature spoke to them in Latin: "Will you call worthless one for whom Christ did not disdain to die?"

The influence of that idea is incalculable. A king does not stoop to pick up a brass ring. When a king stoops to pick up something, it must have value. When Jesus dies for someone, he must be worth dying for. And he died for everyone, says the New Testament. If we would ever let that idea catch on, let it really get started, something is bound to happen to the estimate of man. How any Christian, for whom Christ died, can belittle and degrade any other man, for whom Jesus also died, is too much for me to grasp.

The idea has caught on—a little. Christianity has failed miserably in many ways, but at its best it has reached out to those whom the "learned world" has treated as worthless creatures—the wicked, the neglected, the poor, the uneducated, the exploited . . . *even the learned*. Christian faith believes in the value of personality and the dignity of human life in all forms. At the fountainhead of this stream of faith in man that we call Christianity is that insistent appeal:

The cross, where man is at his worst, has, more than any other influence of all time or any idea, made man believe in his best. As Paul put it: "Where sin abounded, grace did much more abound" (Romans 5:20). That is a strange paradox. Surely there must be something real, potent, saving, victorious at the center of what Jesus did to achieve a consequence like that. If that is what Jesus left the Mount of Olives to confront Jerusalem with, I believe afresh in God.

Later, after the Triumphal Entry, after the week of confronting Jerusalem, after the Passover and the Last Supper, Jesus went back to the Mount of Olives, to the Garden of Gethsemane. There he prayed: "If it be possible, let this cup pass from me." That prayer describes the situation of every one of us. Each of us here is praying to be spared something, if possible. Charles Kingsley, a 19th century English preacher, used to lean over the pulpit in the little village church of Everly on Sunday morning and say: "Here we are again to talk about what is going on in your soul and mine."

That's what I want to do each Sunday, and hope to do, but often wonder if I really do. But at this point I am sure that something is going on in us right now that cries out with Jesus: "If it be possible. . . ." Whatever it is, I don't know, although I do know enough about some of you to know very explicitly what it is. The thing is, can we add that "nevertheless" that Jesus added?

One of the most exciting things I've heard in a long time is the contemporary folk-rock-opera, *Jesus Christ,*

Superstar. I sat one afternoon alone with my dog and listened straight through for an hour and twenty-seven minutes. It is great! It was a religious experience for me, full of emotion. Perhaps the most haunting section is "In the Garden of Gethsemane."

So, when we stand at the beginning of what is called Holy Week: Jesus coming from the Mount of Olives to confront Jerusalem and returning there to pray before the betrayal, arrest, trial, and crucifixion, we find ourselves part and parcel of the scene. We have had our Palm Sundays when all was well. We have had our agonizing days of confrontation. We all face some kind of Gethsemane. All of this is a test of our faith, our character, our loyalty.

An old Hindu quatrain says:

> Like one who doubts an elephant
> When seeing him pass by,
> And yet believes when he has seen
> The footprints left, so I.

Had I been at Calvary, I may have been one of the doubters, one of the deniers, as Peter was. I don't know! How futile that sacrifice, how final that failure! But now—*see the footprints left!* Pilate gone. Caiaphas gone. Empire after empire gone. And the world still turns to that one who did not disdain to die for every man, who kept on loving when he was unloved, who forgave when he was reviled, who let loose in the world the mightiest lifting force that man has ever seen . . . Do I dare doubt that *now,* or deny it? No, I cannot!

So, I want the Mount of Olives to remind me of

the depth of prayer—communion with God, the grace of triumph, the courage to live, the Gethsemane that says "nevertheless," and see the ascension of Christ to the top place in my life.

CHAPTER ELEVEN

MOUNT CALVARY—GOD IS STILL IN CHARGE!

MATTHEW 27:32

"And when they came to a place called Golgotha . . ." (Matthew 27:32)

The exact site of the crucifixion of Jesus is unknown. Although we call the place Calvary, that name is used only by Luke among the Gospel writers (Luke 23:33). The others use the name "Golgotha," which is either Aramaic or Hebrew, meaning "skull." The Greek New Testament uses the word "kranion," which also means skull. The word Calvary is derived from the Latin "calvaria," which also means skull. Calvary is the generally accepted term for the place of Jesus' crucifixion.

Calvary was evidently an elevation, but at a height of some 18 feet it could hardly be called a hill, much less a mountain. The New Testament writers identify it as being on a rather well-traveled road outside the North gate of Jerusalem. If the archaeologists ever locate the line of that north wall, maybe an inscription will be found which will eliminate the mystery. But for now there are two major places that are identified as Mount Calvary.

A fourth century tradition has the site inside the

present north wall of Jerusalem. It is covered by the Church of the Holy Sepulcher, which was begun in the year 325 A. D., following the visit to Jerusalem by Helena, the mother of Constantine. (Helena is responsible for the location of many of the traditional biblical sites. Although her identifications came sooner than those of anyone else, the modern tourist gets the feeling that she found a lot of things that were never lost.) Modern archaeology has a better technique for identification.

The present Church of the Holy Sepulcher is shared by six different Christian groups. Inside the structure is a sort of knoll some 14 to 18 feet (depending on which source you read), rising to the balcony level, and it is called Calvary.

The term "place of the skull" may have sprung from the shape of this incline, from the actual skulls seen in ancient times on this site, or from a legend that the "skull of Adam" was buried in this place. A grotto under the Chapel of the Syrians, which is a part of the church, contains tombs which are said to have been in the garden of Joseph of Arimathea.

The other site is known as "Gordon's Calvary," first seen in 1849 by Otto Thenius and later excavated by Gordon in 1883. This is a small hill outside the wall of Jerusalem and is somewhat skull-like in shape, with "eye-socketed" caves on the side, and adjacent to a garden with burial tombs. To many, this site seems better to fit the New Testament description, especially the tomb area, and it is far more reverent. I first saw this place in 1955 and from a good perspective took pictures which, by using the imagination and allowing for the erosion of centuries, can certainly be seen to resemble a skull. A bus station (which ruined the view) was later built there by the Jordanians.

The emphasis of this chapter will not be the crucifixion of Jesus that took place on Calvary. That was but a part of the total story of Jesus' life which climaxed with the Resurrection. What I want to emphasize is the theme:

"God Is Still In Charge!" And God has the last word.

The Resurrection

Dr. Theodore Clark, former professor of theology at the New Orleans Baptist Theological Seminary, in his book, *Saved By His Life*,[1] brought attention to a facet of the Christian faith that is too often neglected—the resurrection. Of course, the crucifixion is important; so is the birth. In fact, it is impossible to separate any event in the life of Jesus and say, "This is it!" To use a figure of speech: "We cannot put a spotlight on any one part of Jesus' life; we must put a floodlight on the total event."

It is easy, and somewhat natural, for us to put central stress on the crucifixion as the major part in the atonement. One Baptist theologian uses words which are generally used by most:

The final revelation of God was made at the cross; everything else in the New Testament record is subordinate to this central event. [2]

As for me, I cannot agree that the crucifixion was "the final revelation of God." Life, not death, is a final word of God. God has not spoken his last word on any subject, nor landed his last hammer blow on any task. The crucifixion was a vital, and necessary, part of Jesus' work. But the resurrection points out that the crucifixion was not the final act, nor the final revelation. There was more work for the risen Lord to do.

If the New Testament stresses any one part of Jesus' life as being more climactic than another, it is the resurrection. But even this does not say that the resurrection is any more important than the incarnation or the crucifixion. It is to say that the birth and death are incomplete without the resurrection. In fact, there would have been no New Testament, no Christian church, had it not been for the resurrection. The cross would have remained an obscure and meaningless event apart from the resurrection. It was the resurrection that made the difference, that brought the birth, life, and death of Jesus into the proper perspective, "The Total Event."[3] Nothing less could account for the complete change in the lives of those dejected, dispirited men. Nothing else could have sent them out to turn a hostile world upside down. In the New Testament, the resurrection is no appendage to the faith; it is the faith!

The message of Easter is this: that in Jesus Christ the eternal God is still in charge and has the last word. After sinful man had done his worst, thought he had finished up things in his own neat little way—with fear, hatred, jealousy, and the skill of his tools, hammer, sword, and spikes—*God acted!* The sign of the action of God was the reappearance of Jesus. Unmistakably, clearly, as a living reality, Jesus appeared. That, in brief, is the resurrection story. God has the last word, and the Christian faith maintains that God still has, and forever will have that last word.

Do not ask anyone to explain the resurrection, for he cannot. But God's power was at work. Something happened, and Christ lived again—*and he still lives!* In the spirit of the reality of the living Christ, I want us to see some of those last words that God has for us.

For one thing, today's words speak of skepticism, cynicism, and doubt, but the word from God is *faith*.

One of the grave dangers facing our generation is the attitude that no matter what we do, no matter how hard we work, it will make little difference in the sum total of life. Man is so thoroughly sinful, so downright wicked, human nature so depraved and unchangeable that we can never expect it to be any better.

Well, no doubt, there is plenty of evidence about man's evil. Let us never minimize that. Christian faith never does lose sight of the fact of sin. But man's sin is not all that Christian faith sees. We must never lose sight of the fact that Jesus taught that human nature, when redeemed by the grace of God, is capable of building a veritable kingdom of God on earth. More than that, Jesus saw this possibility in some unlikely individual people. He saw a mighty apostle lurking in a cursing fisherman; an angelic personality in a woman of the streets; a spiritual giant in small-statured Zacchaeus, and he saw Paul, the missionary of love, in Saul of Tarsus, the intellectual exponent of persecution. Not only did Jesus see these possibilities, he had faith that something could be done about them.

You see, we do not have to wait until the end of time for that kind of faith to become a part of our personal or collective life. This is not "old school" liberalism believing in the inevitable progress of man, although there is firm belief in the improvableness of man. This kind of faith can become a part of our daily life when the reality of Jesus breaks in upon us and becomes the focal point of our life so that we make the principles by which Jesus lived the guiding principles by which we live.

If anyone ever had the right to feel that cynicism was the order of the day, Jesus did: dedicated to the will of God, seeking only that which was right, going about doing only that which was good. Yet, see how he was persecuted, despised, rejected, and ultimately put to death. But Jesus' faith was in God. And because of his faith in God, Jesus had faith in man.

This kind of faith is the resolution to stand, or fall, by the highest and noblest of ideals. This kind of faith enables a Martin Luther to say: "Here I stand! God help me; I can do no other." This kind of faith is the confidence that, somehow or other, right must triumph over wrong, because God is just.

A new world lies out in front of us—one of the most exciting worlds that man has ever seen or known. But what kind of a world it becomes depends upon where we want to go, what we want to find, how we face it, and what we make of it. It is faith that makes the discords of today the harmonies of tomorrow. What we admire so much in Christopher Columbus is not so much his discovery of a new world; rather, it is his having gone in search of a new world on the basis of his faith in the rightness of his opinion that there *was* a new world out there.

As Christians, with faith in the rightness of Jesus

Christ, we face our world, look for something better, and do something to make it better because we believe a new and better world *is* out there.

A second word from God would tell us to practice *hope* instead of despair.

Hope vs. Despair

Heaven knows, and so do we, that there is plenty of cause for despair in our world. The secular press media, the writers of literature and drama, the artists and musicians have barraged us for two decades about causes and consequences for despair. There is breakdown, tension, and disintegration at every level of life, including the church.

On the other hand, possibly never in history has there been a period that offers more constructive opportunity than right now. Transportation and communication have put us in instant contact and given us knowledge of the world and its people. Technological advances in medicine, agriculture, and education have taught us that we can handle disease, feed people, and erase illiteracy. Even the restless turmoil of the peoples of the world—and our people at home—should be viewed as an opportunity to provide some more answers, not a despairing pessimism that feels futility about problems.

If any of us are alive a half century from now, and many of you will be, the world will be unrecognizable, just as today's world would not be believed by one who lived in "The Gay Nineties." (And in the 1890's the word "gay" didn't mean what it means in the 1970's.)

I believe that those who face tomorrow with faith and hope will be more at home in tomorrow's world than those who face it with cynical despair.

One unforgettable Sunday a man named Fred
Anepohl came to church for the first time able to hear
without his hearing aid. For twelve years Fred had
battled deafness. In all those years there was hope, often
when there was little reason for hope because medical
science hadn't been able to break through. But one day
it did. One of the choice incidents of that situation
came from young Calvin Smith who said: "If Mr.
Anepohl can bring his transistor to church, why can't
I?"

Even those who believe in total depravity, the complete sinfulness and worthlessness of man, preach a
faith that says that in Christ there is hope.

Can you imagine what a poor, shriveled thing life is
without hope? No wonder history has called the day
of the crucifixion "Black Friday." No wonder the disciples were forlorn. All their hopes were shattered.
Their dreams were gone. The bottom had dropped
out of their lives. Their stiuation, as disciples, did seem
hopeless.

If you could but eavesdrop on some of the personal
counseling situations that any minister or counselor
faces in trying to help clear up some muddled lives,
despair seems to be the order of the day. If you could
sit with some lawyers and doctors and teachers and
realize that these are people, persons—not just a great,
big, impersonal, anonymous world—then you would
know the necessity of the word *hope*.

Suppose we were to withdraw the hope that some day
the cause and cure of cancer will be found? Why, it's
that hope that keeps cancer sufferers going.

Suppose there was no hope for the poor and illiterate?
Suppose there was no hope of forgiveness to hold out
to the sinner?

The resurrection changed all that. Despair can be thrown off. Now we can live on the basis of faith and hope as two of our most prized possessions. In the resurrection, after sinful man had done his worst, God spoke.

What gives moral value to hope, what makes it a virtue, is that in its bright forms it is a real act, a striving of the will, an effort of the moral nature.

Hope is an evil if it makes us lazy, indifferent, complacent, or callous. Hope is an act, often a difficult act, of choice and will. Hope is the refusal to be borne down and cowed and depressed by the presence of evil, no matter how dominant evil may seem to be. Our lives in our world is the place where we put hope into action.

There is one other word of God: replace hatred with *love*.

Love vs. Hate

Ah, what hatreds there are in the world. Nation against nation, race against race, class against class, people against people, religion against religion. Because of such hatreds we are often limited in where we can go and what we can do—here at home and abroad.

During World War II, one of the early criticisms of highranking military men about the American soldier was the difficulty in teaching him to hate the enemy. It took an all-out effort on the part of the news media to stir up our civilian population. That was thirty years ago! See the troubles we had in creating a war kind of hatred about Vietnam. The classic expression came from Cassius Clay (Mohammed Ali), like him or not: "I ain't got nothin' against them Congs."

On the whole, we Americans are a gregarious people. Give us half a chance and we'll be friendly with almost anyone. It is distressing to see rising resentments growing up in our midst. Nothing has ever so divided us against each other as did the war in Indo-china.

When Jesus set before his disciples the principles of loving even one's enemies, he presented a terribly difficult task. Why, it's hard enough to love one's friends! It is not always easy to love. Those who have suffered most at the hands of opposing forces may logically have just cause not to love. But, oddly enough, we often find demonstrations of love and forgiveness on the part of those who have suffered more than from those who have not.

But, maybe this isn't so odd, after all. Jesus said that when suffering came for his sake and the gospel's, there would be blessedness as a part of life.

Today's life ought to show us the practicality of what Jesus taught. It's quite obvious what hatred leads to— eating away at our inner being and destroying our outer society. The demands of our day seem to confront us with an ultimatum of understanding and practicing Christian love, else we will live within and among the chaos that hate brings on.

Cynicism and despair never lead to love; they are breeders of hate. It is faith and hope that lead to love. Why? Because both faith and hope recognize, along with cynicism and despair, that there is wrong, evil, and sin. But they refuse to believe that evil is more powerful than right. Not only do Christian faith and hope refuse so to believe, they actively practice what they do believe.

Some people seem to take a morbid delight in the gory details of some juicy, scandalous affair, saying,

"That's the way people are. What else can you expect?"
Love may talk about it, but love tries to understand and
bring about correction. You see, love is never glad when
a person goes wrong. The contrast between love and
hate is seen in such biblical admonitions as: "If a
brother fall . . . if a brother be overtaken in a fault
. . . bear one another's burdens . . . restore such an
one." Hate takes great delight in proclaiming the fall,
the guilt, and demands conviction, judgment, and punishment. Whereas love takes the opportunity to lead
the offender to repentance, offers him forgiveness in
Jesus Christ, and guides him into right living through
another chance.

Now, let's go back to two things—the resurrection of Jesus, and the reality of a new life for us when
the living Christ becomes a part of our life and re-
lives in us.

When a person becomes a Christian, there is a resurrection in his own life—old things pass away and
are put off; we put on a new life. Faith and hope remain
as words of God, but they assume secondary positions.
Love now takes the place of primary importance. There
may be a kind of faith and hope without love, but true
love that is Christian leads us to an unselfish faith and
hope. Love is the divine reality and vitality that everywhere produces and restores life. To each of us the love
of God that is in Jesus Christ can become a part of us,
giving us the power to work miracles—*if we will!*

Whether we can call this little 18-feet incline a
mountain or not, I want Mount Calvary to remind us
that these words of God are more lasting than the words
of men. The resurrection reminds us that God has not
given up on man. To me, a profound idea is not that

God *could* send Jesus back; it is that God *would* send him back at all. Why should he, when men had rejected Jesus? God did not give up on man, either in cynicism or despair. If God had faith and hope enough in man to raise up Jesus and send him back, how can we refuse to have a similar faith and hope? If God loved enough to keep on giving us chances, how can we keep on rejecting that love?

The subject is "God Is Still In Charge!" Let me tell you how I came by that. At the Baptist World Congress of 1955 in London I heard an eloquent Negro preacher, Dr. William Holmes Borders, of Atlanta. His sermon was moving along exceptionally well when, all of a sudden, he shifted gears and began to speak in the inimitable style of the oldtime Negro preacher, moving from Genesis to the Revelation and most points in between. I shall never forget his description of the crucifixion:

"There on top of the hill called Calvary were three crosses with three men hangin' on 'em. Jesus was on the middle one, with a thief on each side. Down at the bottom of the hill is Death, mounted on his scrawny ol' gray hoss. Death looks up, sees Jesus and says, 'That's my man! I' better go get him.'

"He digs his spu's into the hoss's flanks, waves his hand, and shouts: 'Cha'ge!' and he goes galloping after Jesus.

"But half way up the hill, God holds out his hand and says: 'Woah, hoss! Hold on, Death! I'se still in cha'ge!'

"One of those thieves looks over and says, 'Jesus, don't forget me.'

"And Jesus says: 'Son, we'll get together in Paradise. You go on, now, and I'll be there myself 'bout three o'clock this afternoon.'"

NOTES

1. Theodore Clark, *Saved By His Life*, The MacMillan Co., New York, N. Y.
2. Boyd Hunt, *Encyclopedia of Southern Baptists*, Broadman Press, Nashville, Tenn., Vol. I, p. 92
3. Clark's phrase, repeatedly used.

CHAPTER TWELVE

MOUNT OF TEMPTATION—GOD OFFERS A WAY OUT

MATTHEW 4:1–11; I CORINTHIANS 10:1–13

". . . the devil took him to a very high mountain." (Matthew 4:8)

Strictly speaking, there is no Mount of Temptation that we can locate in the New Testament. The Gospel writers use the word "wilderness" in identifying the place of Jesus' temptation. At the time of the third temptation Matthew does say, ". . . the devil took him to a very high mountain."

Jericho, at the time of Jesus' baptism, was a favorite winter vacation spot for high-ranking Roman authorities and Jewish officials. Situated 825 feet below sea level, Jericho is one of the oldest continuously inhabited sites in the Holy Land. Some archaeologists say it was inhabited 8,000 years before Christ. There is a copious water supply there, despite the barren desert surroundings, which makes for lush agriculture and fruit. Herod the Great chose Jericho for his winter capitol. Excavations have uncovered his luxurious palace with its baths, mosaic floors, wine cellars, and the like.

Modern Jericho is a rather squalid little town. It is beastly hot in the summer—the only time of the year that I have been there. But it is interesting, for there

you go to the Jordan River to see the traditional site of
Jesus' baptism and to the Dead Sea.

The surrounding area is almost totally barren—
nothing but rocks—enough rocks to feed the world, if
those rocks could be turned into bread. There are
several high places, mountains, if you please. One of
them is pointed out as the Mount of Temptation. It
is called Mount Quarantina. It is situated in a turmoil
of rocks amid the bleak beauty of extreme desolation
on the edge of the Judean wilderness. The mood one
gets is that of extreme isolation and loneliness. And
there is a monastery on the top.

The first time I was there was in 1955, and I was
alone. I was asked if I wanted to climb the Mount of
Temptation. Being young, I was tempted, but the 120-
degree temperature soon won that argument, and I did
not climb. There has been regret ever since.

Even if there is no specific "mountain," at least something happened there that can be of benefit to us. I
want us to see it under the theme: "God Offers A Way
Out."

Many things about the creation of the universe may
bother us. There are many things we do not understand
about the book of Genesis. But this one thing seems
sure—the writer of Genesis certainly knew people and,
more importantly, he knew God, and he knew how to
get the message of God to people. We are like the people
he knew, and we need the same message of God that
they needed.

Listen to chapter one:

So God created man in his image, in the image of God
created he him; male and female he created them   (Genesis
1:27).

Then turn quickly to chapter three and read:

And when the woman saw that the tree was good for food (understandable), and that it was pleasant to the eyes (she had aesthetic tastes), and a tree to be desired to make one wise (by this time Eve had convinced herself that she would suffer a cultural lag if she didn't get that fruit), and that it was in the center of the garden (temptation is always so central that we cannot escape its fascination), she took of the fruit thereof . . . and gave unto her husband . . . and he did eat . . . And Eve became the mother of all the living (Genesis 3:6).

What strikes us right off is how little space the writer leaves between the story of creation and the story of temptation. Eve's story is the picture the writer had of human life. He had seen enough to know that her experience mirrored yours and mine. This is the story of every man. And the early church dramatized it under that name, *Everyman*.

Our first experience is to be born—to be created. But we do not get very far from the cradle before we have another and equally important experience— choosing between right and wrong. The pattern is as old as Eden:

Chapter One—*Creation*

Chapter Three—*Temptation*

As we come into our theme there are two things we need to get clear at the outset.

For one thing, temptation is on all levels of human life. Temptation is not limited to sex, alcohol, and gambling—to the young or old—the educated or uneducated. It besets us all. When I hear someone say, "I'm too old to be tempted," I remember a humorous little rhyme:

King Solomon and King David lived merry, merry lives,
With many, many lady friends, and many, many wives.
Till old age crept over them and then with many qualms,
King Solomon wrote the Proverbs; King David wrote the
    Psalms.

We might well wish that we would someday get to
the time and place where we could escape having to
make moral choices. But it will never be so. Nor will
we ever be able to limit temptation to any one area of
life, for it always threatens us at all points, even our
strong points. There are childish levels of temptation,
levels of the flesh, and of the temperament and spirit,
all of which involve much agony. No one of us can tell
what another's temptation might be; maybe not even
our own. All we can say is that *we will all be tempted,*
time and again, and often we will yield.

The second thing that needs to be said is that temptation is not the entire problem of morality; it is really
just the second half. The first half of the matter is that
of having moral insight. Temptation implies that there
is a choice. There is either a reasonable or a dramatic
contrast between black and white, right and wrong. If
the whole world is just a dull gray, a matter of all things
being relative, and there are no true, meaningful choices
between good and evil, then, there are simply no temptations, or, at least, temptations become limited.

What I am saying is that in every moral situation we
first have to see that there is a choice and that we are
free to choose. But seeing there is a choice must come
first.

It is at this point that many of us are lacking. One
modern writer describes one of his characters as having

". . . an average little conscience." No moral struggle,
just a day-by-day drifting with no real choices. Or, as a
recent newspaper Chuckle of the Day put it: "Conscience is the still, small voice in every one of us, but to
too many it speaks in an unknown tongue."

The person who is tempted is to be congratulated,
for it shows that he does have some moral insight. But
here is where the real problem arises. Seeing that
there is a choice to be made, how do we find the power
to choose the right over the wrong, the better over the
poorer, the higher over the lower? It is this factor
which makes temptation a real, live issue.

When we are tempted, how can we win? How can we
come out victorious? Out of moral conflict and choice,
how can we achieve moral victory? What are we to do
with temptation? Is there a way out?

In the tenth chapter of Paul's first letter to the
Corinthians there is a verse which gives us a clue to the
answer:

No temptation has come your way that is too hard for
flesh and blood to bear. But God can be trusted not to allow
you to suffer any temptation beyond your endurance. He
will see to it that every temptation has a way out. So that
it will never be impossible for you to bear it   (I Corinthians
10:13, J. B. Phillips).

Paul was writing to people who had to make choices
every day. The contrast between the pagan and the
Christian was dramatically obvious. Theirs was not so
much the problem of finding moral insight as it was
the problem of finding the power to choose the best,
once they saw it. In this sentence Paul gives them, and
us, an assurance, an answer.

First of all, Paul suggests, *when you are tempted do*

not think you are an exceptional case. In the King
James Version the first part of the verse reads: "There
hath no temptation taken you but such as is common to
man."

One of the most characteristic of human traits is that
which causes us to make an exception of ourselves. King
Saul in the Old Testament issued an edict which said
"No witches!" Then, when he got in trouble, he said,
"Find me a witch." I know doctors who say, "No
chiropractors; they must be outlawed." Then they get
down in the back and, knowing there is nothing seriously wrong, say: "Find me one."

Is it not easy when the problem of moral choice
faces us for us to say some things such as:

No one ever faced this particular problem before. It's
different with me.
Oh, under ordinary circumstances a man shouldn't cheat
and steal. Of course not! But this is not ordinary; this is a
final exam . . . this is business.
Under ordinary circumstances a man shouldn't get drunk,
but after all, our fraternity only has its big bash once a
semester . . . our class reunion . . . our annual convention.

Exceptions!

Thou shalt not commit adultery is a sound bit of advice.
But our love is different. People just don't understand the
pressure we're under.

Sit in my office awhile, and you'll learn what pressures
they are under *afterward,* even in the day of "The Pill."
Then choose your pressure!

And so it goes. Put this down as a good rule—Every sin is prefaced by the words, "I'm an exception!" There is a cute little story about a wee girl who was being corrected by her mother for swearing. When she said she learned the words from her daddy, her mother answered, "But Daddy is Daddy." To which the little charmer replied, "Well, I'm *I'm!*" The exception!

Paul is wise in reminding us that when we face temptation we should start by saying to ourselves, "Look, this is old stuff, common to every man." This is how Jesus faced the matter when Satan was trying to convince him that he was different.

"Command these stones to be made bread. Bread, man, the kind you eat! Others can't do this, but you can, that is, if you are really God's Son you can; you're different."
"Cast yourself down from this high place. You're God's 'Golden Boy'; the rules don't apply to you."
"Bow down and worship me. That's forbidden, of course, but God will make an exception in your case in return for all the support I can throw your way."

But Jesus answered: "I'm no different. These temptations are as old as these hills."

Paul goes further to suggest that when you are tempted *always remind yourself that you are never alone.* Says Paul: "God can be trusted not to allow you to suffer beyond endurance."

We must never forget that in the hour of trial we are never alone, especially the Christian, for God is with us. But there is something more. Not only God, but for the most part, fellow Christians are with us, too. Maybe we do let them down sometimes, even as there are some

cases when it seems that our fellow Christians let us
down. After all, they, and we, are human. You see,
there is a sort of cosmic quality in every moral struggle.
I am involved in yours, you in mine, we in each other's.

The eleventh chapter of Hebrews tells us of the
invisible witnesses who surround us, saints of the
household of faith. Then the twelfth chapter begins:

Wherefore, seeing we are compassed about with so great
a cloud of witnesses, let us lay aside every weight, and the
sin which does so easily beset us, and let us run with pa-
tience the race that is set before us, looking unto Jesus the
author and finisher of our faith   (Hebrews 12:1).

The scene is a Roman race track. In the colosseum,
high on both sides, are those who have fought their own
battle for moral character, and they are rooting for us
to do better than they did.

Now, isn't it true that many of us conquer our temptations because we know that someone very dear to us
is in this struggle with us, and we dare not let them
down? We do have invisible witnesses—father, mother,
a loved companion, friends, children. We are a part of
those whom we love. And the fact that they are there
and do love us makes a difference. We are the worst
sort of ingrates if we "let down" those who love us and
sacrifice for us. Does the fact that God is there, Christ
the Saviour is there, make any difference? Of course it
does. There was Joseph, tempted by all the feminine
wiles of Mrs. Potiphar, not totally innocent himself,
saying: "How can I do this great wickedness and sin
against God?"

Listen to the words of a hymn:

I would be true, (Why?)
For there are those who trust me.
I would be pure, (Why?)
For there are those who care.

How dare we be or do anything that is not in the manner and spirit of Christ, *on any issue at any time?*

There is one other thing Paul says: "God will see to it that every temptation has a way out." Naturally, this does not mean that God offers us an easy means of escape, that every situation has a "Deux ex machina," a God of the machine which the Greek dramatists used as an easy way to solve their dilemmas. What Paul says is this: *In every temptation, in every moral choice,* God gives us an alternative, and the alternative is the way out. But we make the choice, not God.

This means that every temptation to evil is also a temptation to some sort of good. Too often we think of temptation as being one-sided, always to do wrong. But every moral choice is double. There are two choices, not just one. There is always an alternative to evil. You don't have to do evil, you know. This is God's means of our escape, the way out.

Think carefully and you will see this truth. You don't have to lie or cheat; you can be honest and tell the truth. You don't have to debauch your life with lust, illicit sex, drunkenness, or drugs; you can be clean, wholesome, and sober. You don't have to rule God out and have done with the church; you can make a time and a place for God at the very center. You don't have to be an irreverant, intellectual agnostic; you can be a reverent, intelligent Christian . . . you can even be a

"Christian Agnostic," as Leslie Weatherhead says, not knowing all the answers, but believing that there are some answers somewhere, if you look hard enough.

This is why the Christian faith is such a realistic affair. The person who is never tempted is morally anemic. He may never do any harm, but he may never do any good, either. Why not find integrity of character and self-control within the framework of faith, rather than in loose living that disintegrates character?

We can go through life always responding to and regarding temptation as something negative, to flee from, to fear. If we do, it is certain that we will lose every time. But Paul knew there was another way to look at temptation, and we need to learn what he knew. In the long run of life, the most alluring, the most tempting things are the good things of life. They have the final fascination.

The name of Dwight L. Moody stands high on the pages of Christian history. He built the Northfield Schools from money he received in his evangelistic campaigns. On a certain hill, they say Mr. Moody wanted to build a chapel. With his typical sense of humor he called the place "Temptation Hill." When asked why, he replied: "Someday, someone just won't be able to resist building a chapel there."
And today on that spot stands one of the loveliest chapels in all of New England.

So, what to do with temptation? Don't consider yourself exceptional. Remember, you are never alone. God always provides an alternative, a way out. But we must have the spiritual discernment to make the right choice. On our own personal Temptation Hill we can raise a chapel to the glory of God.

So, I want that Mount of Temptation to remind us that, despite whatever temptations we may face, God has a way out, an alternative.

CHAPTER THIRTEEN

MOUNT OF BEATITUDES— CHARACTERISTICS OF THE KINGDOM OF GOD

MATTHEW 5:1–11

"And he opened his mouth and taught them, saying, Blessed . . . . (Matthew 5:2)

Wordsworth, in his poem, *The Character of the Happy Warrior,* asks:

Who is the happy warrior? Who is he That every man . . . would wish to be?

Who is the happy person? Who understands the secret of living? What kind of person do we wish to be? Poets, philosophers, and preachers in every generation have asked and answered these questions in a variety of ways.

I believe that the Beatitudes, found in the opening section of Jesus' Sermon on the Mount, offers us the best answer.

Seeing the crowds, he went up on the mountain, and when he sat down his disciples came to him. And he opened his mouth and taught them, saying, Blessed . . . (Matthew 5:1–2).

Thus begins one of the most dramatic, revolutionary, and paradoxical discourses in the annals of man. As the scene of the teaching is a mountain, it is reminiscent of

Mount Sinai and the giving of the Law of Moses. A further comparison to Sinai can be seen as Jesus explains the difference between the old law and the new covenant: "It was said to them of old time . . . but I say to you . . . ." Even so, Jesus also said: "I have not come to destroy the law, but to fulfill it."

Unfortunately, I have been unable to find an adequate description of this mountain. The Bible scholars seem to ignore its location. However, it is in the Galilee region, one of Jesus' favorite places. The mountains around Galilee are beautiful, and the area has a kind of serene atmosphere. Looking across Galilee toward Capernaum there is a height called Hatin, which is generally identified as the scene of the Sermon on the Mount.

As was his custom, Jesus had gone up the mountain, probably to get away from the crowds for a little while. After all, a man does need some solitude occasionally to replenish himself. The constant giving out drains a person, no matter what his field. He has to have some time to take in. On this occasion the disciples went along, and it is to them—probably with the crowd eavesdropping—that the words were spoken. The best known sections of the Sermon are the Beatitudes, the Golden Rule, and the Lord's Prayer.

The Sermon on the Mount pictures the ideal life of the real disciple. It is concerned with righteousness and the New Life of the Kingdom of Heaven. Basically, the New Law is the law of love. Jesus did not present this New Law as a new set of specific commandments to replace those of Moses. Instead, he spoke more about attitudes which carried the idea of voluntarism—internally motivated action, rather than obligation—externally imposed action. He taught that the test of a person is not what has been done or omitted being done, but character is what the highest aspirations are. This higher righteousness is not attained by having a larger quantity of good deeds, but is the result of a life that is transformed by the grace of God.

The first part of the Sermon is a series of sayings which we call The Beatitudes. The word "beatitude" comes from a Latin term *beatitudo,* found in the Vulgate translation of Romans 4:6, meaning "made happy." Since the time of Ambrose, 380 A. D., the term "Beatitude" has been used to describe these clear-cut statements of Jesus in which he depicts the qualities, virtues, or experiences that characterize a citizen of the Kingdom of Heaven.

"Blessed" has become a rather sanctimonious, piously musty word which doesn't appeal to us. The best word we have come up with as a substitute is "happy," and that's not a very good word, either. Happy suggests a too light-hearted, frivolous state to convey the full idea. Happiness seems to depend too much on things that happen to us. What Jesus is talking about is more the kind of character, the inner qualities that enable us to transcend and live above whatever happens to us.

The Greek word *makarios*—the word Jesus used—is not usually translated "happy." Rather it signifies the attainment of life's highest good. Yet, we cannot really separate blessed and happy. Someone said:

To talk about being blessed without being happy is like announcing a hymn without starting the tune.

Some thirty years ago, I had an old friend in Baton Rouge. His name was Dr. E. L. Scott, emeritus professor of Greek at Louisiana State University. A life-time study of the Greek language, both classical and New Testament, had led this Baptist scholar-deacon to believe that the best translation for the Greek word *makarios* was "divine approval." I like that. It is as if Jesus is offering congratulations, the highest accolade, to the person who is living the kind of life he is describing. In fact, the "blessedness" spoken of in Romans 4:6 is a kind of imputed—credited to—righteousness that comes from God. What more or better from life could we ask than the congratulations, the approval of God? Is that not what Jesus meant in the parable when he concluded that God would welcome certain ones by saying, "Come, you blessed of my Father, inherit the kingdom prepared for you." Those who inherit any kind of kingdom are 'approved' ones.

Biblical scholars do not agree on whether Matthew or Luke is the earlier or more accurate account of what Jesus actually said. Nor do the scholars agree as to the number of the Beatitudes. Matthew lists seven or ten, depending on how you count, while Luke has only four (Luke 6:20–22). Matthew states his in the third person, and Luke uses the second person. Both appear to have come from a common written source. While the Beatitudes are grouped together in both places, it is likely that they were spoken separately and repeated at various times for emphasis when Jesus found it convenient to describe the characteristics of the ideal believer.

We have a tendency to read the Beatitudes and the Sermon on the Mount and then try to reproduce the quality of character that is described. When we find that to be difficult, we tend to give up, feeling ourselves to be failures, for the standards are too high and the demands too great for us. What we fail to see is that we just can't do this on our own, without some help. The Beatitudes are not rules we must keep, and in keeping them enter the Kingdom of Heaven. They are illustrations of what happens after—and sometimes a long time after—we are in. For someone outside the grace of God to suppose he can ever rise to the heights of these characteristics is impossible. No wonder Christianity is considered impractical or hopelessly idealistic. First of all, we must settle the problem of "Sovereignty" in our life. That is, who is to be God? Who gets our allegiance? And to have these characteristics, according to Jesus, that sovereign must be God. This takes us back to Mount Carmel and reminds us that this "Who is to be God?" question constantly confronts us. I will return to this idea later.

The Beatitudes—A Paradox

Something strangely paradoxical is seen in the Beatitudes. Jesus actually says that the happiest of all people are those who are generally accounted to be unhappiest of all.

Here was the Greek, entranced by the lore of the ages, worshipping beauty and art, stressing reason and a balanced intellect, making the highest good consist in a life enriched with all the treasures of knowledge and experience. And Jesus said, "Blessed are the poor in spirit."

Here was the Roman, insolently proud of his conquests, his laws and government, his road and water systems, his empire, thinking that life's highest good consists of power. And Jesus said, "Blessed are the meek."

Here was the Jew, believing himself chosen of God, chafing under the heel of Rome, rapt in his dreams of nationalism, envisioning a return to David's kingdom, feeling that the good life was made up of special privilege. And Jesus said, "Blessed are the persecuted."

From the beginning of human history there have been convictions that blessedness is found in prosperity, in long drawn-out enjoyment, in freedom from sorrow, pain, humiliation, and suffering. And Jesus said, "Blessed are the mourning ones."

No wonder he sounds simplistic, impractical, and idealistic.

Yet, who dares to say that the way of the Beatitudes is not thrilling? The thing is, do we dare apply them to ourselves and risk the resultant explosion? Will we allow ourselves to be poor in spirit or meek? Can we be peacemakers? How about those who revile and persecute us; can we bless them? (We may bless them out!) Can we show mercy? Such questions can be answered in the affirmative only if God has become sovereign in our lives. Then we can know the approval of God.

There are four Beatitudes that are common to both Matthew and Luke, although stated in different forms. Those who are blessed, who have the approval of God, are: the poor in spirit—the ones who hunger and thirst after righteousness—the ones who weep and mourn.

This chapter could take different directions: a brief treatment of each Beatitude, found in Matthew, or a larger discussion of those common to Matthew and Luke. Which is better—a little bit about all of them, or

more about a few? Let's deal with only the first
Beatitude and allow it to be representative of the inner
quality of life. Then we will conclude by returning to
the matter of who is to be sovereign of our lives, for that
is the crucial issue.

The Poor in Spirit?

So, the first Beatitude:

Blessed are the poor in spirit, for theirs is the kingdom
of heaven   (Matthew 5:3).
Blessed are you poor, for yours is the Kingdom of God
(Luke 6:20).
Those who do not have a spirit of haughtiness are divinely
approved, and the kingdom of heaven shall be theirs   (as
Dr. E. L. Scott would say).

Whoever heard of any kind of a kingdom going to
someone who is poor in spirit? We naturally expect a
kingdom—political, economic, sports, music—to go to
those who have ambition, who have worked hard and
attained. Here Jesus is saying that the finest of all
kingdoms will go to those who are the direct antithesis,
the very opposite, of what we consider to be success. So
we'd better take a look and try to understand what
"poor in spirit" means.

Of course, we want the kingdom of heaven. Isn't that
what being a Christian is all about? If it is to be given
to the poor in spirit, then we'd better be poor in spirit.
But how—how does one become poor in spirit? Is it
available for our appropriation? Is that something with
which we are born, or can it be achieved? Maybe some
of both. It could even be that the desire and effort to be

poor in spirit might keep us from becoming that way.

Luke says, "Blessed are the poor." Surely, Jesus could not have meant to set down as a principle that poverty in itself is a blessing or that only the materially poor can have divine approval, not when he himself had some wealthy friends. No one knew any better than Jesus how debasing poverty can be. Maybe Luke meant that poverty need not be a hindrance or a barrier to happiness, that some may even miss happiness by the abundance of things in which they seek to find it.

Matthew makes it plain that it is neither a man's possessions, nor his poverty, that matters; it is the spirit of the person that makes for happiness. Any one of us knows that it is as likely for the poor to have the same spirit of grasping selfishness that is condemned in the wealthy. I've seen enough to know that. So Jesus goes beneath the surface and bases the character of the citizen of heaven not upon actual poverty, but upon a kind of spirit of detachment.

Yet, even detachment can be a snare. Sometimes we may get so enthralled with this idea of detachment from things material, and a readiness to do without them (sometimes in what we say in an effort to be Christlike), that our lives take on an "other worldly" aspect, becoming unreal.

There is a lot to be said on the favorable side about some of the current "detachment" movements, especially among the young who discredit material things, live a simple life, communing with nature, being satisfied with a little, and all that. But I see an awful lot of materialism in much of this, and not any more "poor in spirit" attitude than at the opposite level. They do take money from family. They often ask for material things from those who have them, and then look with disdain at their benefactors. This bothers me, and I'm getting "up-tight" about it in reference to asking from the church, receiving, then ignoring the church.

My "fourth-year-at-the-University of Tennessee" son was home recently. He went to the Repertory Theater one night. It costs $4.50 admission, but if you take a copy of the Vieux Carré newspaper, which has a very, very small ad, you can get in for $1.50. Said my son, "That's for the freaks who can't afford it. Only you old folks can afford $4.50." To which I replied, "The old folks can't afford it either, because they are supporting you freaks. Get me a paper!"

There is a drama about the tribulations of an aristocratic English family facing social revolution. At one point in the second act, the eldest son faced his father and delivered a shrill diatribe against the "establishment." He made it quite clear that he was ashamed of his antecedents, disgusted with his class, and wanted nothing to do with his old man. "So far as I am concerned," he concluded, "you no longer exist." The father took this with admirable British calm, and when it had ended, asked quietly, "That's all very well, but how do you propose to live?" The young man threw back his shoulders, thrust out his chin, and replied, "I shall simply have to learn to get by on my allowance." [1]

Most of our difficulty stems from the word "poor." How can Jesus expect us to have characteristics like those which define that miserable word: destitute of property or material things of life; destitute of such qualities as are desirable; worthy of pity or sympathy? But there is a fourth definition in the dictionary: "Free from self-assertion, not proud or arrogant." That sounds more like Jesus.

I suppose what it boils down to is whether or not we are humble enough to receive the grace of God and then not become proud of our humility. Pride is so basic a sin that it can poison even our virtues.

When a person becomes proud of his purity, he becomes a prude. When he prides himself on his correct behavior, he becomes a prig. When he becomes proud of his righteousness, he is like the Pharisee, who thanked God that he was not like other men.

You see, even the Publican's humility can be carried to the point of being spoiled. Like that little grammar school girl I read about, whose teacher was giving a questionnaire to discover which pupils needed special attention in developing social attitudes. To the question: "Which student in the class brags least about himself?" this little girl wrote in her own name. No wonder St. Jerome said: "Beware of the pride of humility."

This Beatitude, with its implication of detachment from the world, has taken on a kind of "other-worldly" aspect. However, I do not believe that Jesus meant for us to be poor-spirited—not with the likes of Peter, James, and John as his closest associates. The poor-spirited person is beaten before the fight starts. He lacks persistence and moral courage. These are serious defects of character and we have a right to condemn such defects. Jesus did. A Christian just can't meet life that way. If anyone imagines that Jesus taught his followers simply to accept the world as it is and risk nothing to make it better, he imagines wrong. The Beatitudes need to be read, along with the complete Sermon on the Mount, especially that section about Jesus' followers being the salt and light of the world.

The poor in spirit are not complacent about their

good points, but they do keep them under control. They keep their consciences sensitive by constant comparison with Jesus. In his presence, they see something more dynamic than mere decency and something more redemptive than mere respectability. In such contrite hearts God can dwell, and theirs is the Kingdom of Heaven.

Earlier something was said about the difficulty of practicing the Beatitudes or living the Sermon on the Mount. The indication was that this was because we are not acquainted with the preacher of that Sermon. The words sound good, and we say that's what we need. But they are impractical and impossible until we have some personal knowledge of him who said them. It's hard enough even then. This leads us back to another earlier premise about who is to be sovereign in our lives.

The first requisite for being blessed, or happy, is to settle the seat of sovereignty in one's life. Whoever has that place gives the approval. To function properly, we must determine the place of final authority. Jesus made this point quite effectively: "No man can serve two masters" (Matthew 6:24). "If a house is divided against itself, that house will fall" (Matthew 12:25). Not only must life be integrated around some central sovereign authority, but, according to Jesus, that sovereign must be God: "Seek first the kingdom of God" (Matthew 6:33).

To Jesus, God was the center of reference in all things and at all times. He viewed every situation in terms of God. He looked up to God. He so completely yielded himself to God that his wishes were at one with God's. Jesus was therefore in the Kingdom of God and the Kingdom of God was in him as he walked around Galilee and as he hung on the cross.

We, too, can be in the Kingdom of God in New Orleans, in New York, or out in the bayou. All we need to do is to make God sovereign in our lives, to test everything we do by reference to him, to put his interests before all else. Then the Kingdom of Heaven is within us.

The old-time evangelists (and some of the new ones) used to exhort their hearers to "Get right with God!" To many that meant—and still means—merely confessing sin, pleading for forgiveness, and starting with a clean slate. Well, it does mean that—*and more!* To get right with God means that we look to him as the heavenly Father whose will we desire to do, and not as a Santa Claus whose gifts will serve our purposes. It means that we use prayer as a boatman uses a boat hook, to pull the boat to the shore and not try to pull the shore to the boat.

In a sermon that came in the mail there was a paragraph from a textbook used in some graduate school. Neither the book nor the school were identified, not even the subject. All that was said was that the book had no relation to the Bible. But that paragraph was in essence what is being said here:

A sense of security is only possible if one is sure of his place, sure of his ability to cope with whatever may come, and sure of his worth and value. Anyone who believes he must energetically seek his place will never find it . . . If one has to be more than he is to be somebody, he will never be anybody. If one does not realize that he is good enough as he is, he will never have any reason to assume that he is good enough, regardless of how much money, power, superiority he may amass. It is obvious that in our society few people believe they are good enough as they are, and can therefore be sure of their esteemed place. Everyone tries to be more, to be better, to reach higher, and as a consequence, we are all neurotic, in a neurotic society which pays a premium to the over-ambitious search for prestige and striving for superiority. Underneath we are all frightened people, not sure of ourselves, of our worth, or of our place. It is this doubt of oneself, expressed in a feeling of inadequacy and inferiority, which is at the root of all maladjustment and psychopathy.

We can agree that this pretty well describes the human situation. I would take issue with the phrase, ". . . if one does not realize that he is good enough as he is." I think I can see what the author intends, but no one is good enough as he is. That's why Jesus came. At the bottom this description centers in our not having done what Jesus said—settle the problem of life's sovereignty, *with God as Sovereign.*

So, I want that Mount of the Beatitudes to remind us that Jesus Christ came to save us, not to satisfy us. That mountain further reminds us that there are characeristics—inner attitudes—that come only when we accept God's grace that brings about divine approval, causing us to become citizens of the Kingdom of God.

NOTES

1. William Muehl, *Reflections,* Yale Divinity School Quarterly, March 1971, p. 2

In Appreciation

In appreciation of you, my friend,
    Of the sweet and joyous thoughts
As I recall your kind smiles to me,
    My broken heart in little bottles I
                brought.

In appreciation of you, God brings
                to mind
    Numerous times you believed in me
When others said things to contradict,
    That caused me to rock and toss
                like the sea.

In appreciation of you, dear friend
                of mine,
    This poem is written today
In hopes that you recognize the sign
    That it'll reveal all I'm trying to
                say.

In appreciation of you, sister (name)
    Christmas brings thoughts of
                tenderness and love
For the ONE TRUE FRIEND who is
                ever the same
Remember it days are stormy
    or peaceful as a dove.

"In Appreciation"

In appreciation of you, my friend,
   Come sweet and joyous thoughts
As I recall your kind efforts to mend
   My broken heart as life's battles I
     fought.

In appreciation of you, God brings
     to mind
   Numerous times you believed in me
When others said things so unkind
   That caused me to rock and toss
     like the sea.

In appreciation of you, dear friend
     of mine;
   This poem is written today
In hopes that you recognize the sign
   That will reveal all I'm trying to
     say.

In appreciation of you, Sister in His
     name;
   Christmas brings thoughts of
     tenderness and love
For the ONE TRUE FRIEND who is
     ever the same,
   No matter if days are stormy
     or peaceful as a dove.